CREATING INNOVATION NAVIGATORS

Achieving Mission Through Innovation

Sabra Horne

BMNT

Published by BMNT, Inc.
410 Sherman Avenue
Palo Alto, CA 94306

Designed by Anthony Santos

ISBN 978-1-6781-4118-9

Contents

Module 8: Metrics That Matter: Outcome-Based Performance

Foreword

There is a dangerous pitfall in the way the U.S. government and other large organizations operate. You can call it a leadership problem, a training deficiency, or a culture issue, but the fact remains: The entrepreneurial spirit is wilting on the vine in the public service sector. Those with innovative talents too often face the choice of either moving to a more conducive environment that nurtures and cultivates their capabilities or stifling the very skills most needed by their employers. This is your call to action. America doesn't have the luxury of allowing this devastating trend to continue.

Our country's government faces a dizzying array of mission challenges: the incredibly fast development of From the perpetual introduction of advanced new technologies, an ever-increasing and relentless number of daily cyber attacks, sophisticated national security threats via multiplying actors from an array of nations and criminal networks, and rising pressures from failing critical infrastructure, the United States and its allies are at a pivotal juncture in maintaining our competitive edge. Each of these challenges is compounded by an unprecedented global pandemic. Thankfully, you—as a proud member of our nation's workforce—are in a position to help. Yet being able to assist our government's essential work is difficult, and knowing how to best assist, such that our vital work is made easier, simpler, less complex, and sometimes less frustrating, can be confusing.

The answer lies in filling the public sector innovation talent gap—providing the tools and resources needed to connect the right people to the right problems, so they solve these challenges and build an ecosystem of like-minded people around them.

Creating Innovation Navigators is the blueprint for any organization, governmental, military, commercial, or otherwise, wanting to foster a culture of innovation among its existing workforce and identify and retain the people who possess that natural talent. It gives leaders tangible resources for harnessing the passions of their staff and translating entrepreneurial spirit into transformative advances for the organization. And it gives motivated employees a break from fighting the uphill battle of bureaucracy with the tools they need to thrive within the workplace. Our single objective is to build an ecosystem of trailblazers to solve hard problems and do great things in an atmosphere that has traditionally hindered creative thinking.

Understanding innovation, how to use innovation to get our essential work done more effectively, and how to navigate the treacherous waters of bureaucracy is not a simpleton's game. Often, innovation is looked upon as a simplistic and ineffective way of approaching difficult work, as superfluous behaviors that get in the way of doing "the real work." Our collective experience in senior government, military, and executive roles has informed this evident truth: that fostering innovation will be the deciding factor behind America's future. The stakes could not be higher. Using the skills of innovation can help make our work easier—and better. We've used these lessons learned to accomplish remarkable things, in remarkably challenging situations, similar to the ones you face today. With this book, we are bringing you into a fellowship of disruption and pioneering growth. We ask that you suspend disbelief as you become a partner in the innovation process described for you here. Given the right tools and renewed priorities, America is destined to awaken a golden era of innovation. Join us. We know these techniques and approaches can help you achieve some amazing results, and we are excited for our country as you begin employing these new skills. We're pulling for you—and our nation.

Pete Newell
CEO, BMNT, Inc.
Austin, Texas

Introduction

Welcome to *Creating Innovation Navigators*, the tool that will help you achieve mission impact in your organization. This book is intended to assist government and public sector leaders in driving innovation within their agency, whether you are trying to bring about innovation within your existing organization, have been asked to be part of an innovation team, or are standing up your own innovation effort.

Creating Innovation Navigators can be used as a reference to accompany any of the BMNT innovation course offerings, as a supplement to your learning within the course or as a stand-alone reference to guide you in your innovation journey. The topics we cover within this book are suitable for any government and public sector agency, including Department of Defense (DoD) organizations; intelligence community (IC), law enforcement (LE), or homeland security (HS) organizations. The framework provided here is methodology-agnostic, meaning you can use it with any methodology (such as agile). And the examples provided within this book cover a wide range of existing innovation efforts and are applicable across government and the public sector.

Our goal with *Creating Innovation Navigators* is to ensure you realize true mission impact by bringing innovation to your organization, not just engage in interesting innovation discussions with your colleagues. We care about getting important, meaningful, and relevant work done—and helping you to do so, as well— so have created a reference tool you can use on your path to innovation, regardless of your particular area of expertise or level of experience.

Creating Innovation Navigators covers basic topics within innovation: how to build innovation organizations, the necessary functions and resources for innovation, ways to measure your progress and metrics to show real change and impact within your organization, and how to communicate your successes. Most importantly, we provide a framework to guide you, the Innovation Pipeline, which gives innovators a common language and process to achieve innovation and mission impact within their organizations, regardless of existing methodologies.

A number of features within this book will help you better understand core innovation principles, lessons learned, and frameworks to approach your own work. Each of the book's eight modules contains **use cases** gathered from top federal innovation efforts that provide examples of successes you can emulate in your own work. Each module also features **key takeaways** that highlight major points in each module. Modules end with **exercises** to give you real practice in building your own innovation efforts; these exercises build upon the work you've done in previous modules. The book ends with an extensive set of **appendices**, which provide you more detailed procedures to build and measure your Innovation Pipeline; a **glossary** to help create a common innovation language; and **resources** for further study.

This book is the result of the contributions of many people over many years. First and foremost, the founders of BMNT, Pete Newell, William Treseder, Jackie Space, and Joe Felter, had a strong vision about how to support the Department of Defense in solving their hard problems and showed remarkable fortitude over the years in achieving that vision. Without their formative military experiences, the hard knocks they experienced along the way, and their research into how to both accomplish mission-driven goals and formulate a better way to accomplish missions, neither BMNT nor the concepts for the Innovation Pipeline would exist, and the ideas included in the book would never have come to fruition.

This book is also the result of the work of many individuals who helped bring the BMNT and Innovation Pipeline vision to fruition, including Anthony Santos, who designed this handsome book; the BMNT Customer Success Team, including Drew Gorham and Vanessa Zabala, who crafted literally dozens of documents to capture the BMNT perspective, many of which appear in the appendices and throughout the book; and the Unmanned Task Force support team, led by Ellen Chang and consisting of Nick Ueng, Donna Ye, and Anders Ericcson, who created the course framework that served as the initial foundation of Creating Innovation Navigators. Key BMNTers, including Steve Blank, Steve Weinstein, Mark Peterson, Conor McClintock, Steve Spear, and Terri Vanech, contributed important intellectual property that has been included in these pages. As author of this book, I am humbled by all that has gone before and appreciative of having the opportunity to unify these ideas into Creating Innovation Navigators.

Finally, we give thanks to the U.S. Navy's Unmanned Task Force and the seminal organizations in its standup as the genesis for this book. It is their heroic efforts to bring innovation to DoD that inspired us to craft a book that could assist them in their work.

We look forward to taking this innovation journey with you. And we are excited to see how you realize innovation within your own organization.

Sabra Horne
Entrepreneur-In-Residence, BMNT Inc.
Washington, D.C.

1

THE CHALLENGE OF CREATING INNOVATION IN ORGANIZATIONS

1.1 Introduction: What is Innovation?

Innovation is anything new that helps an organization accomplish its mission, from small improvements to processes or policies to successful moon shots. Innovations don't have to be shiny new technologies. Innovation can be used to improve any aspect of an organization, using activities that can be scaled and repeated. And over time, these discrete activities can grow into new and improved organization-wide systems that confidently generate new capabilities.

Fundamentally, innovation is about bringing positive change to an organization: finding new ways to approach old tasks and being willing to challenge the status quo to find better, more efficient, faster, cheaper, or less painful processes that will improve the organization's outcomes. Innovation is relevant to and needed in every government agency and public sector, and is an outcome that every agency and organization worker can embrace. Bringing innovation to an organization can be accomplished in a variety of ways, such as adopting new commercial technologies, finding faster and easier ways to procure that technology, changing policies or even laws to remove barriers, and creating new processes to speed up or otherwise improve the old ways of doing things.

But, ultimately, creating innovation isn't merely about new ways of doing work; it is about the *outcomes*, *results*, and mission *impact* of those efforts that create innovation. If the new technology, acquisition methods or processes, or policies don't result in real and significant mission outcomes, you have only engaged in creating innovation theater the tragic result of government effort and monies spent without real results. Innovation is a characteristic of federal workers who are motivated and united by delivering mission impact for their end users, whether critical infrastructure sector workers, law enforcement officials, human services providers, or intelligence officers and warfighters.

> **Innovation: Anything new that helps your organization accomplish its mission, from small improvements to processes or policies, to successful moonshots.**

1.2 Why Do We Need Innovation in Government and Why Is It So Hard?

Approaches to governmental innovation, regardless of the administration, have historically been piecemeal, incremental, increasingly less relevant, and insufficient. Government organizations weren't built for innovation and often do not either draw a workforce that naturally embraces innovation or foster an environment that promotes innovation. So in order to develop an innovative culture within your organization, you must first be an agent of change.

Striving for innovation can be an important way of rethinking existing organizational approaches and activities to improve overall mission outcomes and to have real mission impact. Influential entrepreneur and founder of the Lean Startup methodology Steve Blank describes the challenge of government innovation in a seminal blog post, "The Red Queen Problem."[1] As the Red Queen in Lewis Carroll's *Through the Looking-Glass* explains to Alice, to get somewhere else, you must run twice as fast. All of

[1]Blank, S. (2017, October 17). *The Red Queen Problem- Innovation in the DoD and Intelligence Community*. Blog Post. https://steveblank.com/2017/10/17/the-red-queen-problem-innovation-in-the-dod-and-intelligence-community/

us in government know how the metaphor applies to our work and how very difficult that work can be.

The mere act of trying to change your organization's culture to accomplish a mission is contrary to the nature of government, one of stability, order, and deliberative speed to weigh important but divergent perspectives and to complete the bureaucratic processes necessary for its sound function. The laws and policies that determine government operations weren't built for speed. Frequently, the technology that underpins government is neither state of the art nor user-friendly.

Another factor that makes government innovation so difficult is that each federal agency has a different culture, way of working and achieving their mission, and language used to communicate. There is no common language used in the world of federal innovation, no standard way of turning innovation into results. This book and associated course are intended to create that common language and way of working to help you use the Innovation Pipeline to effectively turn innovative ideas into solutions with mission impact.

1.3 How Can I Bring Innovation to My Organization?

To create innovation, you must think differently to deliver different outcomes. Your innovation story will be based on the work that you do in this book and this course, building from the research you put into understanding the details of your particular innovation challenge, the relevant circumstances and constraints within your organization, the necessary scope of your solution, the timing required to achieve it, the resources you will be able to summon, and the tools you will build and employ.

One fundamental change often needed to achieve significant results is speed. That may mean increasing the speed of your organization's invention, adoption, and deployment of solutions, to matching or surpass the speed at which threats to your mission are encountered, or it may mean learning quickly from successes and failures to apply those lessons to the next effort. The goal is not to catch up to your adversary, but to render the adversary's investment useless, as we recognize the importance of increasing the cost to them.

FIGURE 1.1 EXAMPLES OF HOW ORGANIZATIONAL DOMINANCE CAN BE LOST

- ❌ FAILING TO ANTICIPATE A CYBER ATTACK
- ❌ BOTCHED RESPONSE TO A NATURAL DISASTER
- ❌ AGENCY DATA BREACH OR RANSOMWARE ATTACK
- ❌ GLOBAL PANDEMIC
- ❌ DECLINING ECONOMIC FORTUNES
- ❌ CASCADING SUPPLY CHAIN SHORTAGES

- ❌ LOSING A WAR
- ❌ MISSING A TECHNOLOGY TRANSITION
- ❌ MISSING NEW OPERATIONAL CONCEPTS
- ❌ LOSING ALLIES
- ❌ DECLINING INFLUENCE IN GLOBAL AFFAIRS
- ❌ LOSING LEGITIMACY
- ❌ INTERNAL/CIVIL CONFLICTS

For those outside of the national security space, innovation is needed to deliver results more quickly to the customer (the public), results that are more customer-focused and that increase customer satisfaction and keep pace with cultural changes. In government, crisis brings a necessary speed to our actions, yet we fail to recognize that we are currently in a moment of crisis, and speed is demanded to respond to the emerging threat.

To foster a culture of innovation, everyone within the organization should be encouraged to bring innovative thinking and ways of working to their job. How might each member of the workforce integrate innovation into their jobs? An organization must change not only at the working level but also at its top levels to effect a cultural change. Organizational leadership must demonstrate their commitment to innovation building it into agency strategies, performance plans, and communications. Leaders can show their support for innovation by the following:

- Including the topic of innovation in their workforce and public addresses
- Including innovation in workforce performance plans
- Creating a work environment that is tolerant of, encourages, and embraces new ideas
- Accepting failure as foundational to learning and accelerating innovation

1.4 Innovation Organization and Innovative Organizations

Senior leaders increasingly recognize that the status quo will not allow us to keep pace with the number and range of internal and external threats we face. Consequently, many governmental organizations are turning to the formal structure of a stand-alone innovation organization, which works across operational and management groups to bring about new ways of thinking and acting in order to face and defeat these threats.

Yet each of us, even if we are not involved in creating a new innovation organization, has the ability to bring innovative thinking, practices, and approaches to our organizations to help them think more creatively about mission challenges and possible solutions. We can help determine where and how innovative thinking can shift our ability to meet mission challenges more effectively without facing the resourcing and organizational construct challenges that accompany the creation of any new office.

FIGURE 1.2 VITAL CHARACTERISTICS OF INNOVATIVE ORGANIZATIONS AND INNOVATORS

1.5 Defining the Innovation Problem

Fundamental to devising the right solution to your innovation challenge is first thinking about the problem you are trying to solve for your organization. What are its challenges, and which are highest priority? How would innovation help to solve these challenges? And, central to these questions, what resources are available to solve them?

You may be tempted to start by brainstorming solutions that can be easily employed without researching whether they will actually solve true mission challenges. However, it's vital to balance the need for achieving a "quick win" against the need for a thoughtful approach, for doing the strategic analysis required. Or you may have colleagues who are "good idea elves," well-meaning and creative individuals who suggest many innovative ideas without regard for the hard and necessary work behind employing and executing those ideas. Similarly, you may have colleagues who are campaigning for a very specific solution to solve a problem they face, yet who may not recognize that the solution fails to solve an organization-wide or high-priority problem or is an outdated or unrealistic solution to pressing current challenges.

FIGURE 1.3 THE CHALLENGE OF USG LEGACY SYSTEMS

TODAY'S LEGACY SYSTEMS	WHERE WE NEED TO BE
Large Platforms	Distributed Consumable Assets
Billion Dollar Platforms	Lower Cost Assets
Best In-Class Features	Aggregation of Mass Good-Enough Features
Fixed Features	Easily Reconfigurable Features
Updates to Systems in Months/Years	Updates to Systems in Minutes/Hours/Days
Human-to-Human Connection	Automated Machine-to-Machine Connections
Hub and Spoke Networks	Mesh Networks
Incumbant Primes	New Primes
Operate our Own Assets	Buy Flexible Services and Outcomes
Waterfall Engineering	Iterative and Incremental Agile Engineering
Fixed Contracts	Agile Contracting
Innovation Disconnected from Lower Echelon Activity	Continuous Innovation Integral to the Mission at HQ Level

First and foremost, any innovation efforts should align with your agency's mission and strategic goals. It's vital to balance the need for achieving "quick wins" against the need for a thoughtful approach to the strategic analysis required for bringing innovation to your organization. Quickly showing progress illustrates to your colleagues that it is possible to rapidly develop some solutions—a critical moment in gaining recognition across your organization that innovation is not just a buzz word, that innovation means quickly addressing mission challenges to devise innovation solutions that will help achieve mission impact.

Don't lose sight of the importance of first developing a strategic approach in creating an innovation organization or developing innovative approaches to assist your organization. In creating your innovation strategy, it's helpful to refer to the foundational documents that define your organization's mission and inform its goals and priorities. There may be a number of artifacts that do so, including leadership and agency guidance and strategies, federal and congressional mandates, and executive orders. Aggregating all such documents will help clarify your organization's highest priorities and provide insights into how innovation can assist it in achieving mission.

USE CASE 1: The Cybersecurity and Infrastructure Security Agency's (CISA) Innovation Hub
Innovation Problem to Be Solved: *How might innovation better support the CISA mission?*

Background:
- Amazing and broad mission: to defend the 4.7 million owners and operators of US critical infrastructure from cyber and physical threats
- Broad authorities to achieve mission
- Strong Congressional support
- Very small workforce to address a mammoth mission
- Although Congressional authorization provided for 30% increase in workforce personnel, challenges exist to hire personnel quickly and in obtaining security clearances to onboard staff
- Cumbersome acquisition processes slowed ability to purchase and deploy commercial solutions or to leverage external expertise

Innovation Solution:
- To meet strategic CISA challenges, use creative means and alternative authorities to bolster the constrained CISA resources to support the CISA mission by:
  - Finding commercial technology used by other USG organizations that meets CISA mission; use alternative DHS authorities and DHS contracting support to purchase and transition tech quickly
  - Finding academic programs to develop and deliver mission solutions that could not be developed by existing CISA personnel
  - Developing alternative acquisition capabilities within CISA using external expertise to speed acquisition processes
  - Creating partnerships with other USG/DOD/IC innovation organizations to learn from them and to leverage their capabilities
  - Bringing about required culture change within CISA

Lessons Learned:
- Building innovation efforts into ongoing programs of record is essential
- Maintaining leadership support, despite government personnel changes, significantly impacts innovation efforts
- Leveraging other programs of record and their resources is vital

Don't forget to include problems within your organization that may be overlooked or that may be hard to discuss with colleagues or leadership. Some potential solutions may be unpopular or even risky to contemplate (such as disbanding an unsuccessful part of your organization or working with an unpopular group to build capacity). But innovation is not for the faint-hearted—only by including difficult ideas in your strategic thinking can you address all of your organization's challenges.

While gathering your organizational challenges, it's important to speak with a wide range of key leaders and workers within your organization. This helps you better understand the context and need for innovation within your organization, the challenges that exist in creating innovation, and, most importantly, the potential for success if innovation is realized. Talk to colleagues in various levels across the organization, especially those who are creative thinkers who see opportunities in many places. They will be sources of insights you would not have had otherwise. And it's also important to talk to those within your organization who are more resistant to change to get a sense of other, perhaps more rigid types of thinking you may encounter in your innovation journey and to discover areas where innovation may be most needed. Having broad input from a wide range of internal stakeholders not only gives you new insights, but also helps you gain buy-in from these early advisors to your subsequent innovation solution.

1.6 Framing the Innovation Strategy

Your innovation organization or the innovative methods you will bring to your existing organization exist within a broader context that is critical to understand to be able to successfully make the required changes. There is a quantifiable environment that is necessary to analyze to best develop innovation solutions. The questions below can help you frame, formulate, and evaluate your innovation strategy.

FIGURE 1.4 FACTORS IN FRAMING YOUR INNOVATION STRATEGY

CULTURE — What are the values of your organization? What are its goals? What does it care about? What does it not care about?

MINDSETS — Is your organization more traditional or does it easily adopt new ways of thinking and acting? Does leadership desire a more flexible and responsive organization? At what levels and where in the organization will you likely face disagreement? Will this disagreement halt or merely hinder your plans?

PROCESSES AND POLICIES — What major processes and policies currently exist within your organization? Are there new processes being developed? Are any of these mandated by legislation? What processes are tossed aside in times of crisis?

OBSTACLES — What are existing challenges to change that will make your journey more difficult? Why do they exist? How might they be overcome? What tools, skill sets, structures, and/or leadership are missing?

OPPORTUNITIES — What are mission challenges your organization could successfully meet if conditions were favorable?

1.7 Staying Alive While Creating Innovation

In tackling your organization's innovation need, you are undertaking important work with the intention of improving your organization, but this role can pose a real risk to you professionally and even threaten your career prospects. Innovation requires courage and risk-taking, often acting at the cutting edge of organizational activities. You will be pushing the boundaries of accepted processes, policies, partnerships, and ways of functioning. Many people are opposed to or afraid of change and so will ignore, resist, or even openly attack your efforts. You may find yourself the source of controversy, subjected to attempts to discredit or delegitimize you and your work with your colleagues going after your resources to defend their own rice bowls, or shut out of daily organizational activities.

Ron Heifetz, Harvard Kennedy School of Government professor, highlights the importance of "staying alive"[2] while leading—that is, not getting fired, being marginalized, or losing legitimacy. Being asked to create an innovation organization for your agency or to create innovative methodologies across your organization may be a thrilling proposition, but it can pose real risk to you professionally. At the end of day, you must be able to stay alive while being an innovation leader. You may be the target of controversy, subjected to attempts to discredit or delegitimize you, your colleagues going after your resources to defend their own rice bowls, or you may be shut out of daily organizational activities, threatening your career prospects. Innovation requires courage and risk-taking, with you and your innovation colleagues often acting at the cutting edge of organizational activities. You will be pushing boundaries of accepted processes, policies, partnerships and ways of functioning. It can be an uncomfortable position, but one with great potential rewards for your organization and for you, both professionally and personally. Chances are you have not built your career on safe bets—otherwise, you would not have been asked to take on this innovation challenge.

With this book and the accompanying course, you can navigate the challenges of bringing innovation to your organization and de-risking activities by thinking holistically and comprehensively about your undertakings, rather than wildly grabbing at actions to make some good things happen.

With these caveats behind you, let's begin our journey.

Module 1 Key Takeaways

- Innovation is anything that helps your organization accomplish its mission, from small improvements to processes or policies to successful moon shots.

- To develop an innovative culture, you must be an agent of change.

- Creating innovation isn't about new ways of doing work; it is about the outcomes, results, and mission impact of those efforts.

- Speed is a fundamental change often needed to achieve significant results.

- A strategic approach is best, whether creating an innovation organization or developing innovative approaches to assist your organization.

[2]Heifetz, R.A. and M Linsky, (2002) *Leadership on the Line: Staying Alive Through the Dangers of Leading*. Harvard Business School Press.

EXERCISE: DEFINING YOUR INNOVATION STRATEGY

What is the central mission of your agency or organization?

_____

_____

_____

What challenges does your organization face in meeting this mission?

1 _____

2 _____

3 _____

4 _____

5 _____

What opportunities exist or lie ahead for your organization's mission?

1 _____

2 _____

3 _____

4 _____

5 _____

What resources exist to aid in your innovation journey?

1 _____

2 _____

3 _____

4 _____

5 _____

What untapped resources could assist in your innovation journey?

1 _____

2 _____

3 _____

4 _____

5 _____

Using these ideas, what is your innovation problem?

_____

_____

_____

What is your strategic approach to solving this problem by using innovation within your organization — how will you achieve innovation?

_____

_____

_____

THE INNOVATION PIPELINE

2.1 Introduction: What is the Innovation Pipeline?

Government agencies often make the mistake of viewing innovation as a set of unconstrained activities with no discipline. For innovation to benefit a company or government agency, it needs to be adopted as a process from conception to deployment. The Innovation Pipeline is a disciplined, repeatable, and scalable means to introduce and manage disruptive innovation within your organization. It is also methodology-agnostic, meaning it works in conjunction with any existing innovation methodologies your organization may already be using. You may already be incorporating activities from one part of the pipeline, but you can benefit from using a more holistic, overarching way to bring mission impact to your organization.

Think of the pipeline as your organization's innovation framework. It is an operating system that develops validated solutions to difficult problems to deliver results as well as mission impact. It helps you to identify where you should maximize or minimize efforts that increase innovation, and it arms teams with the necessary tools to make data-driven, evidence-based decisions to ensure that the right solutions are created for the right problems.

The Innovation Pipeline enables you to gather problems that your organization faces, whether emerging or persistent, identify solutions to those problems, and determine a pathway to solution adoption; it can be used by almost every type of government organization, including those that integrate emergent commercial technologies, leverage academia, encourage workforce crowdsourcing, include makers and builders, use prizes and challenges to deliver innovation, and encourage facilitators in their processes.

The steps of the Innovation Pipeline were developed from helping government organizations create innovation and innovative organizations and from reflecting on our own experiences in bringing innovation to existing organizations. That said, the power of the Innovation Pipeline isn't merely in understanding and performing its steps; it is in achieving the effects of the work done along the pipeline, which is innovation itself.

Note that solutions to problems do not exclusively entail purchasing commercial technologies to be integrated into your organization. Although some innovation organizations focus on transitioning emerging technologies into government use, there are many other viable solutions for tough government problems: new or revised policies, processes, authorities, tools (such as playbooks), resources, communications, and even laws (although these require congressional action). Innovation can be brought to any aspect of government work—acquisition and contracting, funding, security, operations, performance management, and policy, to name a few.

Depending on the type of innovative organization you will be working with (see Module 3 for further discussion of government innovation organizations,) you can employ any number of these possible solutions.

Ultimately, the Innovation Pipeline will help ensure your work will result in real change for your organization.

2.2 Why Do You Need an Innovation Pipeline?

When thinking about how innovation can help your organization, it is easy to abandon a disciplined approach and instead consider a variety of random solutions, using many agency resources in the process. The Innovation Pipeline, a strategically organized end-to-end process from idea to deployment, helps you:

- gather a wide range of issues facing your organization
- focus your energy on addressing your organization's highest-priority problems
- consider a variety of possible solutions to these high-priority problems
- ensure delivery of solutions with real mission impact

By utilizing the steps of the Innovation Pipeline, your innovation efforts will move faster and more efficiently, feeding an increasing number of problems into the system, to help find solutions in a time frame that provides an advantage over your adversaries. It increases the number of opportunities you have to leverage the entirety of your resources. With its bias toward action, the pipeline helps you "fail forward" and thus get to the next potential solution faster. It will also help inform decisions about how and where the organization can change to meet strategic imperatives.

The Innovation Pipeline helps you to

strategically decide which areas of your organization need innovation, implementing a narrowing approach from initial issue gathering and problem sourcing, to discovery, to incubation and transition. At the end of your Innovation Pipeline, you will have determined a limited—not overwhelming—number of possible solutions to help you achieve innovation; the pipeline increases your chances of finding those opportunities. Only the most strategic, desirable, feasible, and viable solutions should warrant your organization's time and resources. The Innovation Pipeline helps you find those solutions.

Most importantly, the Innovation Pipeline provides a unified and common language and set of steps and activities to realize innovation that can be used across government organizations, regardless of their mission. Given the disparate functions and goals of the huge number of government agencies, there is great power in having a unified language and practice that can be leveraged across the entire government for mutual benefit. Current approaches to innovation across the government, regardless of the administration, are piecemeal, incremental, insufficient, and increasingly less relevant in achieving game-changing mission results. Yet the increasing demand for integrating innovation into government work points to the need for a new, unifying approach.

2.3 Why Will the Innovation Pipeline Help You Achieve Mission?

The Innovation Pipeline provides a framework to focus your energies on what to do within each stage of the pipeline. It helps you find the right solutions by trying many problems, and many solutions, that could aid your organization's innovation. By tying in theoriginal organizational challenges discovered in Module 1, the Innovation Pipeline helps you tell a compelling story about

what this process entails, and why. The point of the Innovation Pipeline is to have a process, rather than a series of disjointed and disconnected actions. Without an end-to-end system, organizations are left to rely on innovation by exception (such as luck, genius, or heroics), which is unreliable and unsustainable. Decision-makers need a framework to rapidly prioritize and drive mission solutions.

2.4 What Does The Innovation Pipeline Entail?

The Innovation Pipeline consists of five steps:

1. Sourcing problems
2. Curating and prioritizing problems
3. Discovering solutions to problems
4. Incubating possible solutions to the problems
5. Transitioning solutions into your agency or organization

Although the Innovation Pipeline is a stepwise process, it is also an iterative continuum. Projects may need to return to an earlier step as you discover new information. But as you progress through the pipeline, problems and solutions generally become linear as a team coalesces and matures around problem sources.

In thinking about the five steps, it is helpful to try to achieve three sets of activities within each step:

- What are the inputs required to fuel this step of the pipeline? How can you gather the right information necessary to adequately fulfill the requirements of this step?
- What activities must be engaged in to gain the knowledge required?
- And what outputs are expected in this step of the pipeline?

The following describes in detail each of the five steps of the Innovation Pipeline—the goals of each step, examples of the step, and key questions to ask at each step. For greater detail on the specifics of what each element might consist of within each step, along with resources needed to complete each step, see Appendix A.

For additional specific information on the inputs, outputs, and activities in each step, refer to Appendix B.

FIGURE 2.1 THE INNOVATION PIPELINE

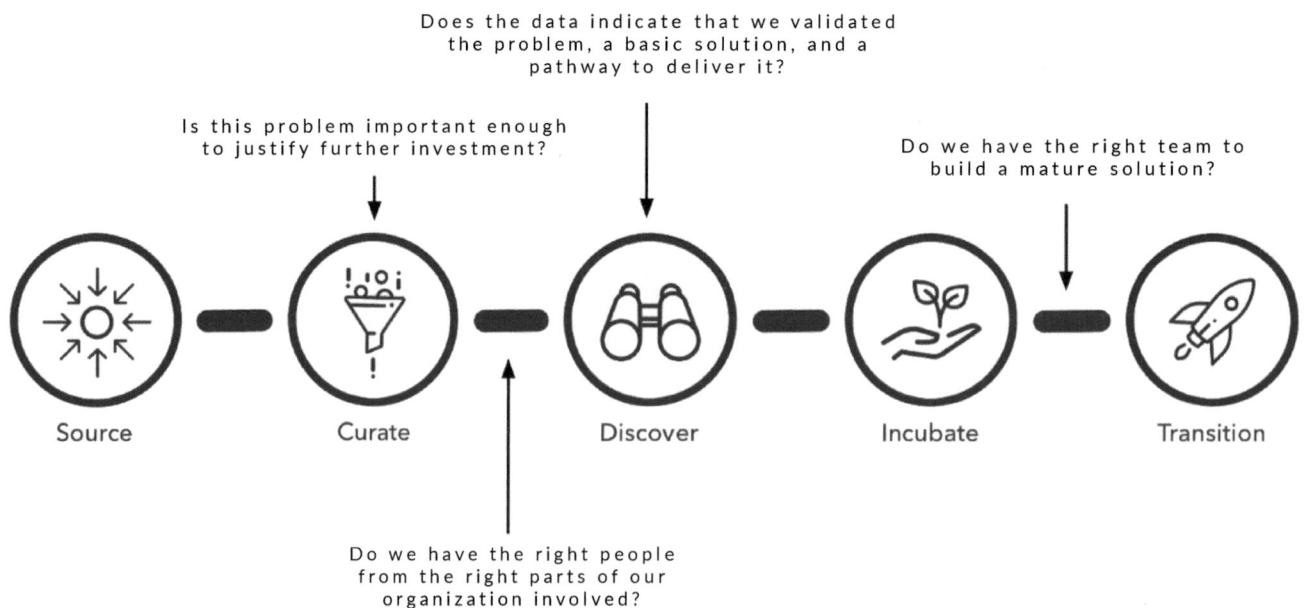

Does the data indicate that we validated the problem, a basic solution, and a pathway to deliver it?

Is this problem important enough to justify further investment?

Do we have the right team to build a mature solution?

Source   Curate   Discover   Incubate   Transition

Do we have the right people from the right parts of our organization involved?

THE
INNOVATION
PIPELINE

 SOURCE

 CURATE

 DISCOVER

 INCUBATE

 TRANSITION

Step 1: Sourcing Problems

The first step of the Innovation Pipeline, sourcing problems, entails discovering and collecting a wide range of challenges faced by your organization. Understanding the problems your workforce faces on a daily basis is the first step toward creating solutions to those problems, and the more problems you collect, the more likely you are to craft successful solutions. These problems are not just those that can be solved with operational technology; they may be policy- or process-focused; they may require new strategies and project teams to be developed; they may depend on creating and disseminating communications; or they may require resource allocation. The problems should be mission focused, whether operational or business processes. They can be sourced from inside your organization, or externally, such as from academic or research communities, industry, or other government entities.

The more problems you collect, the more likely you are to craft a successful solution. There are several ways to solicit problems within an agency, including gathering ideas from workforce crowdsourcing efforts (such as TSA@Work or NASA@Work), holding problem-sourcing workshops to brainstorm problems, using technical means to collect information (such as InsightAI), collecting challenges from existing requirements gathered by the organization, and interviewing leaders across the organization who have been tasked with solving problems within their organizations.

Most important in this process is finding and developing as many sources as possible to ensure that you capture a wide variety of perspectives within your organization. Members of your agency view their challenges differently depending on where they sit in the organization and the type of work that they do, whether mission operational or business process in focus.

Problems can be found in several ways:
- Participants bring their own problems
- Commands or organizations submit their own problems
- Leadership provides problems that appear within the organizations

Regardless of your sourcing method, problems can be solicited either according to a specific "challenge" (for example, "how might we improve our agency's ability to quickly hire new talent?") or by an open solicitation that doesn't limit the focus of the problem. The approach chosen, specific or open, depends upon the needs of your organization, the number of workforce members polled, and the time and resources available to address the problems presented. When sourcing from larger groups, the specific challenge approach can lead to an increased ability to deliver on the problems gathered.

Useful problem statements should include three elements, as the design company IDEO wisely asserts:

- What are the basic components of the problem?
- Who would benefit from a solution?
- What is the basic outcome of a solution?

For more information, see *Appendix C*.

By talking to problem owners, you will gain many insights into the nature of the problem and the pain points. For tips on conducting interviews, see *Appendices E* and *G*. To capture the information you've gathered in your interviews, see *Appendix F*.

Goal for the Innovation Team: Build a repeatable and scalable sourcing process that ensures a fresh pool of ideas, tech, people, and problems that is exponentially larger than the number of solutions desired to be deployed (using internal and external resources).

Goal for Leadership: Understand the challenges that impact the organization's ability to achieve mission quickly, effectively, and painlessly.

Key Questions to Ask: Where are people struggling? What makes work more difficult? What process/policy/tool/resource/technology might help us achieve mission more quickly or effectively?

Examples of Possible Problems

- Staff offices, from Levels 15/14 below, need more rapid and definitive communication from their division and branch leadership to have clarity on their work so they can complete projects faster.

- Chief Information Officer (CIO) employees need a way to identify CIO services, capabilities, and processes and know how to access them, how best to use them, and who is responsible for them, to utilize available resources more effectively and better support mission partners.

- Strike Team Commandos need a transformed mobility training solution to increase the probability of mission success and survivability.

- The Chief Development Office needs a data-tagging framework that describes the handling of data in specific domains to comply with national and local law and policy and to ensure agency data has appropriate labeling and access controls.

- CIO personnel need a clearly defined and consistent requirements process to more effectively vet requirements and to ensure contracts are awarded quickly and correctly.

Step 2: Curating and Prioritizing Problems

Curation involves two basic tasks: assessing and prioritizing problems. In curation, you take the problem areas/problem statements from step 1, sourcing, and dig deeper to understand the true nature of the problems generated. This phase is about finding the true, root problem, which may differ from the problem initially presented, by looking for the cause of the problem and/or assessing the problem against agency or mission strategies. Curation may require more time than sourcing, especially if the problems are of a technical nature requiring development and a concept of operations. But the better you understand your problems and the more you explore what is possible, the more likely you are to solve them.

You can use the "How Might We" model, popularized by IDEO, to reframe problem statements into curious, open-ended questions that more easily allow future possibilities and solutions. For more information on crafting such statements, see Appendix G.

Example: How might we maximize strike team commando driver capabilities?

It's important to understand why each problem was posed, who is affected, how it might have manifested within the organization, and how solving the problem can help achieve organizational mission.

Sometimes, however, your sourcing will produce problems that aren't organizational problems or that aren't mission focused. Not every problem is worth pursuing. Review the following three factors for each problem to determine if it warrants further consideration:

- **Desirable:** Is this the right problem? Is a solution wanted by the end user?
- **Viable:** Is it sustainable in the long term? Is it supported politically?
- **Feasible:** Are potential solutions technologically possible?

If any of these three factors aren't met, a problem may be not worth the expenditure of resources. Interviews with beneficiaries, stakeholders, and advisors who can provide insights can help you answer these questions and decide which problems to proceed with. For more information on problem curation, see Appendix H.

Once assessing has taken place, prioritizing the problems is essential to ensure that your constrained resources are spent on the most important issues, resulting in real mission impact. Prioritization can be done by referring to agency strategic documents, which highlight the agency's highest priorities. These are the documents you used in Module 1 to create your innovation strategy. There may be several different types of artifacts that articulate agency priorities, such as requirements documents, leadership guidance, and federal mandates and strategies. Aggregating and using all such "limiting factors" documents will result in a clear illustration of the agency's highest innovation priorities and provide the necessary justification and evidence of how you prioritized your sourced problems.

To begin the process of prioritizing problems to winnow them down to workable solutions, each problem should be rigorously assessed by its opportunity cost: what resources are required to achieve a solution, and how much of an impact can the solution have on mission? Is this really an important problem? How do you know it is important?

Agency and organizational priorities, strategies, national guidance, emerging crises, and leadership guidance all can provide insight into what can make a difference in mission. Real data—from end users, beneficiaries, and stakeholders—are needed to create quantifiable, repeatable standards. Creating repeatable standards for assessing and prioritizing problems will be important to illustrate the legitimacy of your curation process. To ensure real prioritization, rank problems from 1 to n rather than assigning a priority rating (e.g., 1 = highest priority, 5 = lowest priority), which usually results in most problems being ranked as highest priority.

A host of potential issues will be revealed as soon as you start thinking through your idea. Capture each and try to identify which criterion or combination of criteria best validate each sourced problem: user desirability, organizational viability, or technical feasibility. Note that it's possible for assumptions to blend into two or three categories. Often, problems can be solved at the local level, by connecting to the right entities, directing to existing tools or resources, or coaching on funding or authorities.

Goal for the Innovation Team: Build a repeatable and scalable curation and prioritization process that creates a vetted problem pool that is much larger than the desired number of solutions to be deployed.

Goal for Agency Leadership:
- Create continuous insight into ongoing and emerging problems and the decay of current assets.
- Establish organizational momentum for innovation based on a prioritized portfolio of current and future problems.

Key Questions to Ask: Is this problem solvable? Does this problem already have an existing solution? Is the problem important enough to justify further investment? Will this potential solution make a difference in mission?

Example Problem and Assessment Factors

Proposed Problem: Drivers need a synthetic training course to become better prepared for real-world operations.

Is it desirable: Will a synthetic training environment aid mobility training?
- Tell me about your current driver training course.
- How closely do you think it mimics a real-world operating environment?
- How well does your current driver training prepare you for real-world operations?
- Would you be open to using a simulated training environment if it required you to use a VR headset?

Is it feasible: Do data to build the synthetic environment exist?
- What software have you seen that builds a map based on collected imagery?
- Do we have any satellite imagery or map data in house that can be used to build a simulated environment?
- Have you seen any companies that take these data and build a simulated or immersive experience?
- How do video game companies build a simulated environment?

Is it viable: Can external training enablers be found and funded in time (6–12 weeks)?
- Does your organization have any VR headsets right now that we could use?
- Are you able to buy a software license for quick testing in a sandbox (off-network) environment?
- Are funds available to purchase a software license for a limited duration experiment?
- Who approves requests like this?

Step 3: Discovering Solutions

In the discovery step, you take the prioritized problems from step 2, curation, and develop and analyze potential solutions through research to create a minimally viable product (MVP), a conceptual approach that allows you to test whether the product will meet the needs of end users. Its main purpose is to help you gain a deeper understanding of the mission needs and requirements for each solution. It brings together stakeholders, product experts, designers, software architects, project managers, and policy and legal experts—all those whose combined expertise can offer a holistic view of the opportunities and challenges involved in solving each problem. They will help you gather as much information as possible about the market, the target audience, and the competition.

In this step, you will test and validate hypotheses and assumptions, assessing operational potential, markets, and technology to inform later development. Potential solutions may include appropriately written policies, detailed processes, new proposed authorities, tools (such as playbooks), resources, communications, and even laws (although these require congressional action). Discovery emphasizes the viability of each potential solution—Is it useful? Is it usable?—before investing too many resources, too much time, or too much money. This step helps you find ways to easily and inexpensively test your solutions to avoid spending money on a product that might not be the right fit for your problem. More importantly, you want to ensure that the product or solution is solving a real mission problem for real people.

In the discovery step you will benchmark similar solutions from other organizations or conduct market research and data collection according to the problem data you have curated. Benchmarking is an appropriate activity for nontechnical solutions (processes, policies, documentation, communications.) For technical solutions, market research is required. Most market research is done at the macro level, such as on an industry technology domain from Gartner or another provider. Often, however, that level is too high to be applicable to a real problem. Interviewing and exploring companies in the context of the organizational problem is critical and is often where technology matching (finding technical solutions for problems) goes wrong. Noncontextual industry market research may not be specific enough to address organizational problems; you need market research that is a specific, contextual, and tailored set of solution mapping.

In discovering potential solutions for prioritized problems, consider these steps to assess possibilities for each problem:

- Understand the end user affected by the problem
- Ensure the problem is clearly defined, with outcomes articulated
- Identify potential risks of a proposed solution

There are several ways to understand the end user, the problem definition, and potential risks. "Customer journey maps" are highly effective in understanding the pain points experienced by users and for providing insights into solutions to those problems. Once you've understood the challenges, craft potential solutions to include the project's goals, required timelines, and costs.

Testing of hypotheses and assumptions, as well as potential solutions, should involve real end users to see whether each proposed solution will actually solve the problem it addresses. Again, the proposed solution can take any number of forms—policy, process, tool, or technology—and having feedback from those who will be using the solution is vital in assessing viability. Develop a list of questions that cover your most important assumptions so you can test them now, rather than learn later you were wrong about one (or more) of them. Ask specific questions of specific people. Avoid the mistake of asking people questions outside their area of expertise, causing them to speculate. If done right, your questions will be answered; from there on, you can make calculated decisions about whether to continue to pursue the feasibility.

If, during the discovery process, you realize a proposed solution is not worthy of the needed investment of resources, then pivot away from that solution and discard it as a possible outcome. There are several factors that make the proposed solution not viable (see step 2, curating); as we considered with sourcing problems, those factors are desirability, viability, and feasibility. Is the potential solution sponsored? If not, start exploring sponsors. Validate or invalidate hypotheses, including thinking of the full process and adoption cycle, to include resources and possible solution owners. For more information on creating solutions from your problems, see Appendix I.

Goal for the Innovation Team:
- Build a repeatable and scalable discovery process that validates problems and solution pathways, while also narrowing the number of potential solutions to include only the most viable options for further investment.

Goal for Agency Leadership:
Establish a continuous flow of options to:
- Accelerate the replacement of old or degrading capabilities
- Disrupt emerging threats

Key Questions to Ask: What are potential solutions to this problem? What's the cheapest/fastest/most accurate test I can perform to validate (or invalidate) my assumptions? Do the data indicate we validated both the problem and a basic solution? Are there other viable solutions to this problem?

Step 4: Incubating Solutions

In incubation, you take the early versions of your solutions from step 3, discovery, and build or develop early versions of these solutions and minimally viable products (MVPs). Once hypothesis testing is complete, many projects will still need a period of incubation as the teams championing the projects gather additional data about the application, further build the MVP, and learn to work together. Incubation requires dedicated leadership oversight to ensure that the fledgling project has sufficient resources and a champion to guide it to maturity. The more you can learn, iterate, experiment, test, and improve upon your solution before launch, the more successful your solution will be. Specially developed tiger teams or external partners are required to develop solutions. Funding may be required, if a technical solution, in order to create an MVP. For further information on building the knowledge you need to create an MVP, see Appendices J and K.

In order to enter the incubation stage, proposed solutions should have ample justification gathered during the discovery phase in order to justify the investment of time and money necessary to develop an MVP. Justification includes a high ranking of the problem as detailed in step 2, curation, significant support from potential end users of the solution, market research indicating a need, and leadership support.

If the solution is technical in nature, agencies often have incubator or development organizations specifically intended for developing this type of tool. Their assistance should be garnered, but note that the speed of the Innovation Pipeline demands a common understanding of the time lines and expectations that need to be met before development begins.

A formal "gate" review of the solution should be conducted at the end of incubation to ensure that the solution built addresses the original problem it was intended to solve, aligns with higher-level guidance and strategy, is feasible from a resourcing perspective, and is a desired outcome for end users. For further support, see Appendix L.

Goal for the Innovation Team: Build a repeatable and scalable incubation process: establish a supply of investible solutions matching the number desired to be deployed

Goal for Agency Leadership:
- Show awareness of and visible support for the insertion of new solutions into existing programs.
- Provide funding for incubation teams, active pipeline participation (mentors, coaching, etc.), and continued support.

Key Questions to Ask: Are our early solutions scalable? Can they be delivered? What needs to change before delivery? Is the market ready? Is there support?

Step 5: Transitioning Solutions

Transition takes the developed solutions from step 4, incubate, and integrates them into existing organizational processes and tools to scale the solutions to maturity. With well-curated and clear problem statements, a deep understanding of what technologies currently exist, data that validate your hypotheses, and multiple rounds of iteration, you are now ready to launch your solutions.

The transition of solutions into the agency or programs should be easier because of the previous Innovation Pipeline steps you have taken. End users and stakeholders have been included from the beginning, and you have been seeding the successful integration of the solution for some time. Stakeholders who support the solutions have been identified and provided context for the problems. If the preceding steps were successful, then you have developed a network and solution pathway that facilitates adoption and use of the solution.

In transitioning your solution to the end user, it is helpful to have a common understanding of the solution, the process remaining to transition the solution, and a discussion about this process. Appendix M offers a template for documenting and formalizing the transition, if this is a necessary step for your solution.

Goal for the Innovation Team: Establish a pathway for off-ramping from the innovation team to a transition team, or program a team to manage organizational technology refactoring.

Goal for Agency Leadership:
*   Support insertion of new solutions into existing programs, specifically by providing funding and headcount for new solution insertion.
*   Recognize and manage organizational technology refactoring.
*   Establish guidance for the transition of solutions that fit in the white space between programs (who is responsible for accepting?).

Key Questions to Ask: How do we mature this solution? What do we need to scale our solution? What do we need to do to sustain this solution?

T
R
A
N
S
I
T
I
O
N

2.5 Crafting Your Innovation Pipeline

Before you begin the activities associated with the five stages of the Innovation Pipeline, it is vital to envision your specific pipeline, the activities you will use in each of the five stages, and the people and partners who will help you complete each of the stages. By crafting your Innovation Pipeline, you will gain a sense of the resources you will need to complete the activities. And you will avoid the pitfalls of leaving out one of the critical phases or activities necessary for a robust approach to the pipeline.

Most importantly, crafting your pipeline at the outset of your innovation process provides you a way to communicate to your leadership how you will be realizing innovation for your organization, as well as to communicate to your partners in the innovation process what is required to bring about the desired innovation. Communication throughout the process is a critical component to innovation success, helping to ensure that the organization understands what and why you are trying to achieve and how it will benefit the organization's mission.

There are five distinct elements that create the infrastructure of your Innovation Pipeline (also see Appendix A):

1. The pipeline and infrastructure processes to achieve the inputs and outputs of each step
2. The activities (including inputs and outputs), methodologies, and tools required to achieve each step
3. The data you will track to indicate the robustness of each step
4. The metrics you will gather and analyze to illustrate the performance for each step
5. The operational support you need to execute the inputs and outputs of each step, including funding, personnel, skill sets, contracting support, legal, security, and/or IT.

FIGURE 2.2 THE INNOVATION PIPELINE FUNNEL

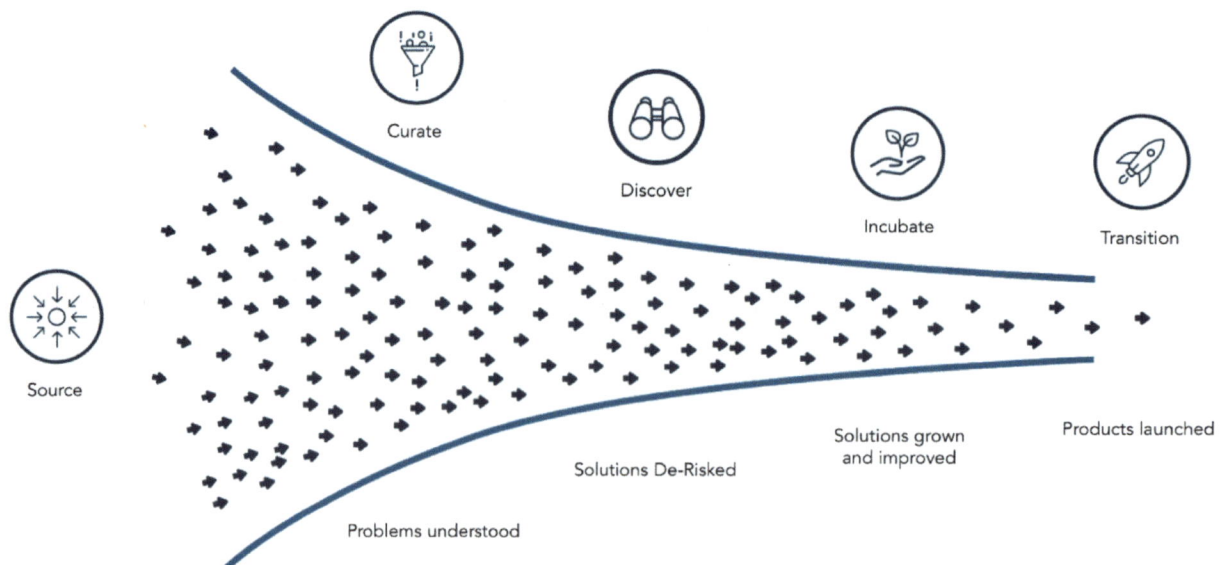

Each of these elements should be determined before you begin implementation of your Innovation Pipeline. Often, enthusiastic innovators want to jump into the more exciting part of innovation, bringing good ideas to life. But a comprehensive and strategic approach in crafting an Innovation Pipeline specifically suited to achieve mission results for your organization will save much heartache, miscommunication, and wasted effort down the road.

You've already successfully crafted your innovation strategy in Module 1 of this book. Crafting your Innovation Pipeline process will consume the remainder of Module 2. You will tackle building your pipeline infrastructure in Module 3. Guidelines for scoping your needs for operational support are provided in Module 6. Methodologies and tools for your pipeline are covered in Module 3 and in Module 6. Finally, metrics to measure your Innovation Pipeline are given in Module 8.

2.6 Pipeline Infrastructure Resources

To successfully complete each of the five steps of the Innovation Pipeline, you'll need to ensure that you have planned and are adequately resourced for each step. As you move through the pipeline, different types of personnel and support are needed at each phase. Support for aggregating and assessing problems are needed in sourcing and curation, market research capabilities are needed in discovery, and technical expertise (such as policy development, project/program management for process development, legal and/or acquisition expertise for authorities and laws, and technical expertise for technical solutions) is required for incubation and transition. For information on resources for the infrastructure of each step, see Appendix A.

We recognize that crafting and executing an Innovation Pipeline as described according to this book is a significant undertaking that requires equally significant resources and, ideally, a dedicated staff as well as focus and resources from across your agency. We are excited that there are already a number of large federal agencies and organizations that are building and fulfilling their own Innovation Pipelines to realize mission impact.

Regardless of the resources you have available for creating an innovative organization, even if you have only one dedicated FTE with no funding (see Use Case 1: CISA's Innovation Hub, which resulted ultimately in a funded program of record), the principles described here can be used to focus organizational efforts on achieving mission results in innovation. But just like in any government work, the more and higher-quality resources you can dedicate to innovation, the better the results you can achieve.

2.7 Natural Attrition in the Pipeline

The Innovation Pipeline process should be robust at the outset to ensure you have gathered enough problems addressing the challenges within your organization. There should be a considerable drop-off in the number of problems that make it from sourcing into discovery and from discovery into transition. Many solutions are valid to solve the problems every organization has, and the pipeline will naturally diminish as you move through each step.

FIGURE 2.3 EXAMPLE OF ATTRITION IN THE INNOVATION PIPELINE

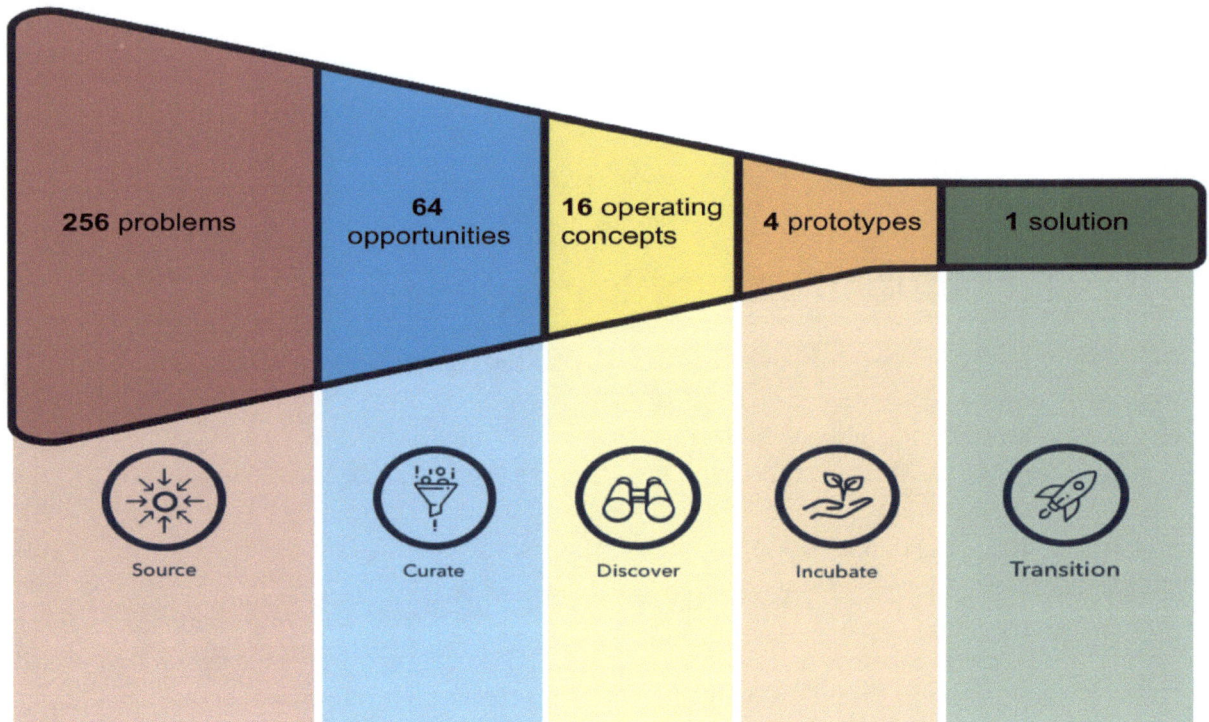

| 256 problems | 64 opportunities | 16 operating concepts | 4 prototypes | 1 solution |
| Source | Curate | Discover | Incubate | Transition |

But also consider the curation and discovery process you've crafted and how you have winnowed a large number of problems into a smaller number of solutions. Be sure you haven't unintentionally scaled back the number of problems so significantly that there are few solutions left to consider. By opening the aperture of the Innovation Pipeline funnel and by making your decision criteria less stringent in the curation and discovery phases, you can ensure you are considering and prioritizing the full range of problems your organization experiences. Conversely, you and the available resources to manage this process may be overwhelmed by the number of problems that remain in the incubation step because you removed only a few problems during the discover stage. If so, make your decision criteria more stringent to ensure that you have a sufficient yet reasonable number of problems and solutions to consider for mission outcomes. For more information on assessing problems and solutions, see Appendix N.

At the end of the day, you are the creator of your Innovation Pipeline, and you have both the ability and responsibility for its care and feeding, adjusting the steps as needed as you learn about their efficacy in meeting mission impact.

2.8 Getting Started in Creating Your Innovation Pipeline

This entire book is intended to help you create, test, and refine an Innovation Pipeline suited to meet the needs of your agency and achieve real results in agency mission. *Creating Innovation Navigators* gives you step-by-step guidance, with each module building upon the work you've done in previous modules, to help you craft your pipeline. In the exercises at the end of each module you will do the work necessary to build the pieces of your pipeline; following the processes outlined in the exercises will get your well on your way. The appendices are intended as a set of resources to help you in refining and assessing your pipeline, providing a greater level of detail for those who are resourced to employ a greater level of effort. See specifically Appendix O to better understand how and when to evaluate your pipeline.

To create your innovation pipeline:

1. Understand your agency's or organization's innovation problem (Module 1)
2. Create a strategy for how you will solve this problem (Module 2)
3. For each of the five steps of the Innovation Pipeline, plan and resource the key elements (Module 3; Appendices A and B):
   - the process to achieve the inputs and outputs
   - the activities (including inputs and outputs), methodologies, and tools
   - the data you will be tracking
   - the metrics you will be gathering and analyzing
   - the operational support required (personnel, contracting support, legal, security, IT, HR)
4. Consider what type of innovation model is needed (Module 4)
5. Map your stakeholders (Module 5)
6. Consider whether you need any additional tools to support your pipeline (Module 6)
7. Build communications with stakeholders (Module 5)
8. Create metrics to measure your pipeline regularly (Module 8)
9. Assess and retool your pipeline as you learn about its efficacy (Appendices O and P)
10. Communicate your successes as you achieve them (Module 5)

Again, not every organization or agency has the resources to achieve the full set of recommendations outlined in this book, and in many cases, not all of these recommendations are essential. Building an innovation effort that results in real mission impact is possible with a more scaled back version of the Innovation Pipeline.

Regardless of your and your agency's stance on innovation, the recommendations and resources outlined here can move you forward on your path to realizing mission impact. You may be part of a mature innovation organization that has already implemented some of these processes; if so, consider how you can use this book to improve the quality and impact of your organization. Your agency may not be interested in building a separate innovation organization to achieve results; if so, what can you learn from this book and what can you employ to improve the ability of innovation to achieve mission results? You may not be in a leadership position that would allow you to implement many of the recommendations here; if so, what can you take back to your organization and your colleagues that will help them bring innovation to your organization?

USE CASE 2: The US Army's Rapid Equipping Force (REF)
Innovation Problem to be Solved: *How might we increase the Army's use of commercial technologies to benefit their mission?*

Background:
- The REF was established in 2003 to accelerate the use of material solutions and technology insertion into U.S. Army elements.
- The REF had an existing rapid response capability to develop, prototype, acquire, and transition commercial and government off-the-shelf solutions to meet urgent combat requirements for deployed forces.

Innovation Solution:
- Established the first Innovation Pipeline to understand mission problems and to identify and transition solutions into existing programs of record
- Solved difficult Army mission problems such as dismounted IED defeat and dismounted operations support; created intelligence, surveillance, and reconnaissance (ISR) capabilities in inhospitable operational environments; and developed force protection and sustainment within a small common operational picture
- Budget was initially $120 million but leveraged the resources of other organizations (up to $1.5 billion in operational costs)
- Outcomes and impact of the REF Innovation Pipeline:
    - 7 portfolios
    - 840 problems sourced and curated
    - 260 problems discovered and prioritized
    - 360 solutions initiated (multiple solutions for each problem)
    - 115 solutions incubated (deployed to theater)
    - 20 solutions transitioned to programs of record

Lessons Learned:
- To be successful, REF required the support of a broad range of skills, including acquisition officers, scientists, and other technical professionals, as well as the ability to reach out to industry and the research community.
- To achieve rapid results, REF needed a single chain of command with the authority to ensure that operators, acquisition officers, and scientists worked together to negotiate adequate solutions to complex problems.
- REF needed access to flexible funding not designated for a specific program to allow the agility to meet mission needs.
- Initially, efforts were focused on transitioning solutions to the field rather than on understanding field problems and needs.
- Direct, unfettered access to Army senior leaders was critical for success in meeting immediate requirements while cutting through bureaucratic red tape.
- $38 million was spent before the REF was able to speed the requirement/acquisition/transition process.
- Doing the work (the activities) in each step of the pipeline was essential to getting the data for making adequate decisions about understanding and progressing problems and solutions and moving them through the pipeline.
- Telling the story of the REF became an essential skill in REF success and sustainment.
- There is a difference between acquiring tools and equipping the warfighter; different skills, resources, and connections are required for each.
- The REF learned to focus the pipeline on solving big problems rather than addressing small hindrances that appeared when problems were sourced.
- • Knowledge transfer was critical to ensure that end user needs and pain points were communicated between the previous supervisor and the successor.

Module 2 Key Takeaways

- The Innovation Pipeline is a disciplined, repeatable, and scalable means to introduce and manage innovation within your organization, resulting in real change.

- The pipeline includes five steps: sourcing problems, curating and prioritizing problems, discovering solutions, incubating solutions, and transitioning solutions.

- There are many types of innovation solutions beyond technology, such as policies, processes, authorities, tools (such as playbooks), resources, communications, and even laws.

- The five elements of the infrastructure of your Innovation Pipeline infrastructure are the pipeline and infrastructure processes; activities, methodologies, and tools; data; metrics; and operational support.

- The Innovation Pipeline process should be robust at the outset to ensure you have gathered enough problems that can address the challenges within your organization.

EXERCISE: MAPPING YOUR INNOVATION STRATEGY TO THE INNOVATION PIPELINE

This exercise will help you map your innovation strategy to each of the five steps of the Innovation Pipeline.

What is your innovation strategy?

_____

_____

_____

_____

_____

How will you source problems to feed your Innovation Pipeline?

1 _____

2 _____

3 _____

4 _____

5 _____

Who will curate these problems and by what process?

1 _____

2 _____

3 _____

4 _____

5 _____

What will be the decision criteria you use for prioritizing problems?

1 _____

2 _____

3 _____

4 _____

5 _____

How will discover a range of possible solutions for these problems?

1 _____

2 _____

3 _____

4 _____

5 _____

What are potential resources in incubating possible solutions?

1 _____

2 _____

3 _____

4 _____

5 _____

Who will assist in the transitioning of these solutions?

1 _____

2 _____

3 _____

4 _____

5 _____

How will these problems and solutions solve your innovation problem?

_____

_____

_____

_____

_____

Notes:

3

INNOVATION
ORGANIZATION
MODELS

3.1 Introduction

Across the U.S. government and in public service, there are many ways to bring about innovation within an organization. In some government organizations, innovation is part of its DNA, the way in which they approach their work. Sixty years ago, when President John F. Kennedy challenged the country to put a man on the moon by the end of the decade, the National Aeronautics and Space Administration (NASA) did, albeit with many painful and costly failures along the way.

Although there are many other inspiring examples of successful government organizations that take risks and try new approaches to get their mission done quickly and effectively, government often has the reputation for being antithetical to the principles of innovation, that is, acting with speed, making swift and informed decisions, pivoting quickly when required, and moving rapidly to new solutions. In inherently bureaucratic environments, some federal organizations are created expressly to achieve innovation, such as the Department of Defense's (DoD's) Kessel Run and the U.S. Agency for International Development's Global Innovation Exchange. And some U.S. government organizations originally intended to drive innovation may have become more bureaucratic over time, given funding challenges or increased commercial capabilities. Organizations such as the Defense Applied Research Projects Agency (DARPA) and the National Aeronautics and Space Administration (NASA) have benefited from leveraging commercial capabilities.

But in general, the necessary building blocks and processes of the federal government can inhibit the speed and action required to drive an innovative organization.

Currently, there is no formal U.S. government organization that unifies and drives federal innovation efforts, nor is there a unifying U.S. innovation strategy or doctrine to articulate a common language and a set of goals and actions required to achieve federal innovation. Rather, individual agencies may create a stated policy or implicit focus on activities across the workforce to create an innovative organization, or they may encourage individual factors for success that emphasize innovation as a core competency. Less frequently, agencies create specific innovation organizations to realize innovation across the agency by modeling, funding, facilitating, or inserting new capabilities, processes, policies, and tools to jumpstart innovation within an agency.

In creating your own innovation organization or in driving innovation across your agency, it is helpful to understand the types of federal innovation organizations that exist so you can explore options for standing up or crafting an approach for your own agency that strategically addresses your agency's strengths, weaknesses, threats, and opportunities (see Module 1).

3.2 Types of Federal Innovation Organizations

Within the federal government, there are over 300 organizations focused on driving innovation within agencies, with many different approaches. Federal innovation organizations and innovation efforts have to date taken six basic approaches:

- Commercial technology acquisition
- Workforce crowdsourcing
- Leveraging academia and research
- Prizes and challenges
- Makers
- Facilitators

FIGURE 3.1 FREQUENCY OF FEDERAL INNOVATION APPROACHES

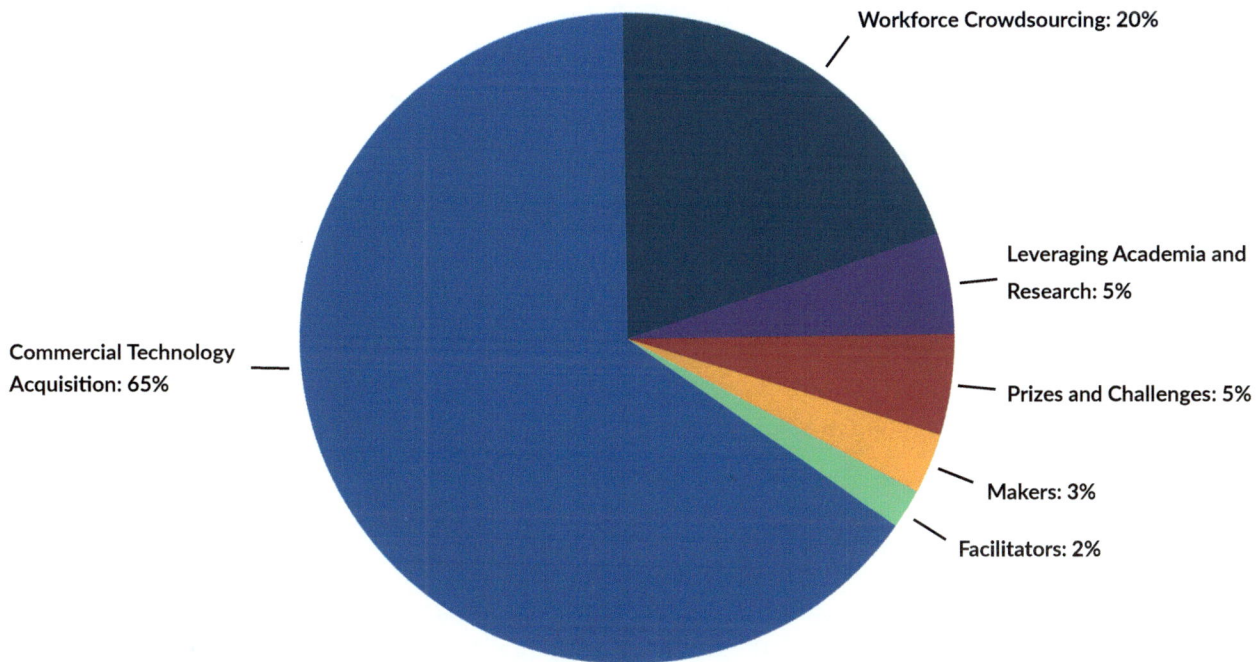

Each of these six approaches is intended to bring innovation to an agency, but each does so in a different way, depending on the mission need of the agency or organization and how the agency has determined innovation can best support the agency mission. Note that three of these six types of federal innovation efforts use talent and resources residing outside of the government to support government work (commercial technology acquisition, leveraging academia, prizes and challenges), which illustrates the importance in innovation of creatively using all available resources and authorities to achieve the best results.

The choice of approach used in federal innovation efforts may depend on the resources available to the innovation organization: who creates the solutions, whether internal agency staff or personnel external to the agency, and where solutions come from, whether they are created within the agency or by external capabilities brought into the agency.

Some federal innovation efforts are primarily focused on creating internal solutions to realize mission results for the organization. Two such examples are the Health and Human Services (HHS) Idea Lab, which gathers problems across its workforce, and the U.S. Immigration and Customs Enforcement (ICE) Innovation Lab, which creates

technical solutions for difficult information-sharing problems.

Some innovation organizations are focused on finding innovative solutions outside of the agency, such as the U.S. Air Force's (USAF) AFWERX, which attempts to find commercial technologies to address mission challenges, and the U.S. Agency for International Development's (USAID) Global Innovation Exchange, which seeks solutions to agency problems from contributors literally around the world.

Federal innovation efforts may use personnel within the organization to solve its mission problems, such as the National Aeronautics and Space Agency's (NASA) NASA@Work program, which asks its own workforce to think about agency challenges. But occasionally agencies can use federal personnel outside of the agency to solve mission problems, like the General Services Administration's (GSA) 10x and 18F, both of which help other agencies solve problems, and the U.S. Digital Services, which similarly works across the federal government to bring about technology solutions.

Let's explore the six common types of federal innovation efforts more deeply.

Figure 3.2 Types of Federal Innovation Efforts

FOCUS OF APPROACH

	FINDING INTERNAL SOLUTIONS	FINDING EXTERNAL SOLUTIONS

CREATORS OF SOLUTIONS

USING INTERNAL STAFF

INTERNAL SOLUTION BY INTERNAL STAFF

Workforce Crowdsourcing:

- HHS Idea Lab and IGNITE Accelerator
- NASA@Work
- TSA IdeaFactory
- USCG Ideas@Work

Makers:

- ICE HSI Innovation Lab

EXTERNAL SOLUTION BY INTERNAL STAFF

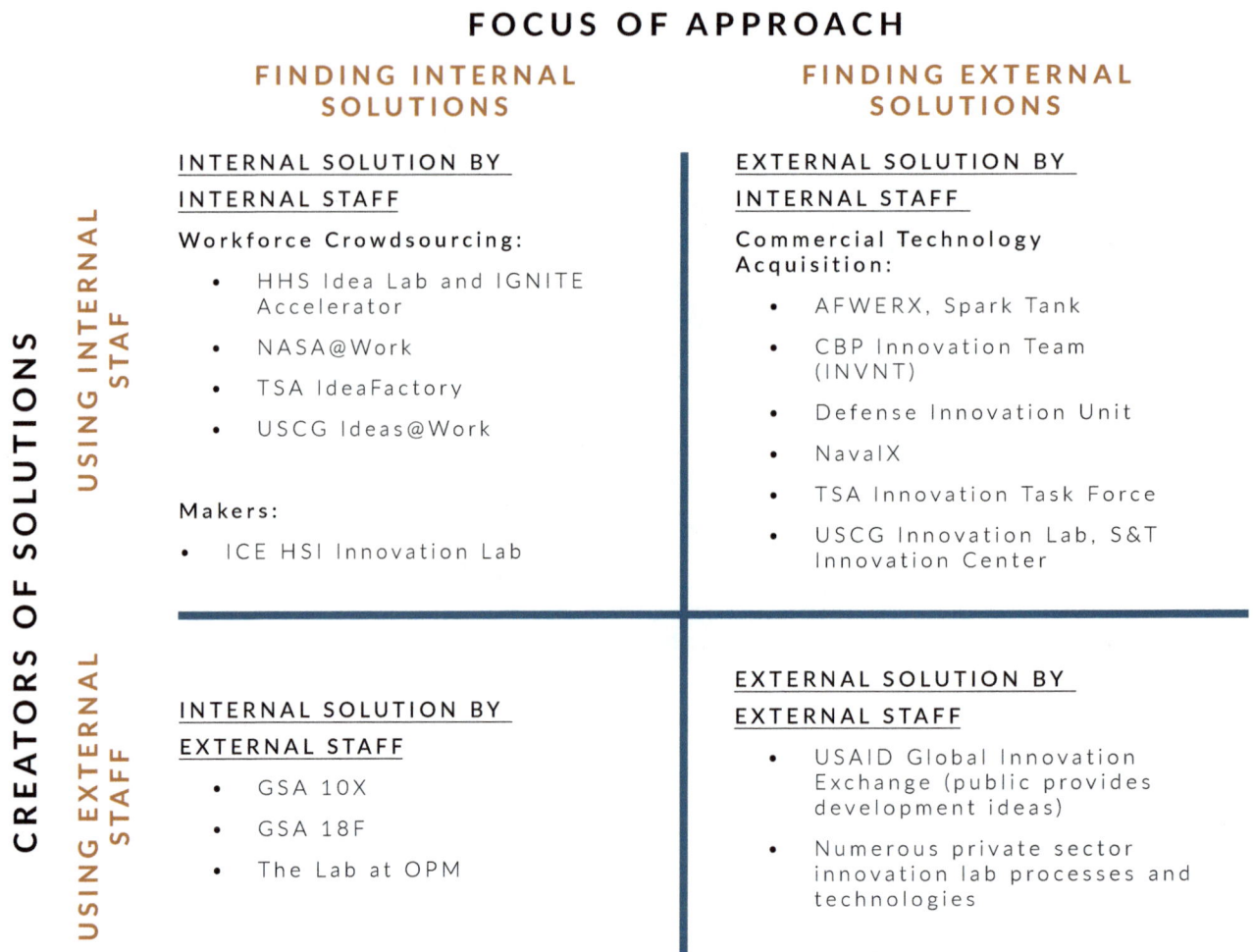

Commercial Technology Acquisition:

- AFWERX, Spark Tank
- CBP Innovation Team (INVNT)
- Defense Innovation Unit
- NavalX
- TSA Innovation Task Force
- USCG Innovation Lab, S&T Innovation Center

USING EXTERNAL STAFF

INTERNAL SOLUTION BY EXTERNAL STAFF

- GSA 10X
- GSA 18F
- The Lab at OPM

EXTERNAL SOLUTION BY EXTERNAL STAFF

- USAID Global Innovation Exchange (public provides development ideas)
- Numerous private sector innovation lab processes and technologies

Commercial Technology Acquisition

The majority of federal innovation organizations and efforts, approximately 65%, focus on finding and acquiring commercial technology to benefit existing capabilities, tools, and systems. The federal government's great need for a wide range of technologies (operational technologies, business process technologies, and information technology) grows each year, but the government is no longer the exclusive source for creating these technologies. Thankfully, many decades ago the federal government recognized that the private sector was creating technology solutions that could be superior products, were refreshed frequently, and could anticipate and even drive the ways in which technology was used.

Unfortunately, the government's ability to quickly acquire and successfully integrate these capabilities has not kept pace with the growing demand. Although there are new and more flexible ways to acquire capabilities (see Module 4.2,

Contracting Authorities and Acquisition), there are still too few to fill all federal acquisition needs quickly.

The DoD is a primary federal agency interested in finding ways to bolster its existing technologies within the services, given its vast size and significant need for cutting-edge operational capabilities to outpower and outmaneuver the adversary. Many complementary DoD innovation efforts focus on leveraging commercial technology, such as the Defense Innovation Unit (DIU), a cross-agency effort, and service-specific organizations such as NavalX, AFWERX, and Army Futures Command; thus innovation efforts focused on acquisition of commercial technologies is the dominant model. Note that many non-DoD innovation efforts also emphasize technology insertion to drive their operational focus, including the Customs and Border Patrol (CBP), the Transportation Security Agency (TSA), and Health and Human Services'

(HHS) Biomedical Advanced Research and Development Authority (BARDA).

These innovation efforts emphasize rapid purchase and transition of technologies into operational capabilities, with a focus on speed, vastly expanding the range of capabilities the federal government has available, and ensuring these capabilities can be used more quickly. Many of these organizations have been provided and successfully leveraged OTAs (Other Transaction Authorities), which can provide greater flexibility by significantly shortening the time needed to award contracts and increasing the interaction with the commercial sector, such that federal contracting needs are better understood and therefore better met by commercial solutions. Some federal organizations have even been created to help the federal government better utilize OTAs, such as the Small Business Administration's (SBA) Small Business Innovation Research (SBIR) and Small Business Technology Transfer (SBTT) offices. Some federal offices, such as the Department of Homeland Security's (DHS) Procurement Innovation Lab (PIL), emphasize leveraging traditional Federal Acquisition Regulation (FAR) quickly and efficiently, while benefitting, when possible, from OTA authorities.

Corollary industry engagement efforts, such as industry days, or leveraging organizations, such as In-Q-Tel, can effectively identify commercial technologies.

USE CASE 3: Department of Defense's Defense Innovation Unit
Innovation Problem to Be Solved: *How might the DoD better acquire and transition commercial technologies across the services to solve critical military problems and directly benefit the warfighter?*

Background:
- Directed by then-Secretary of Defense Ash Carter in 2016, DoD needed to better access technologies created by early-stage startups.
- DoD was no longer setting the standard for most technologies, such as autonomous vehicles and natural language processing.

Innovation Solution:
- The Defense Innovation Unit was asked to acquire, prototype, and transition early-stage commercial technology.
- It was the only DoD organization focused exclusively on commercial technology acquisition and adoption, serving all services.
- Focused heavily on using alternative acquisition processes and authorities (primarily the Commercial Solutions Opening program), with teams of acquisition experts to assist with rapid purchasing and transitioning across the services.
- Encouraged nontraditional tech companies to focus on DoD problems and have them work with Primes
- Able to accelerate time to contract to 31 days.

Lessons Learned:
- By focusing on rapid acquisition, the time to identify, acquire, prototype, and transition a commercial solution to the field can be 18 months or less.
- By gathering requirements at the highest levels, significant national security challenges can be addressed.
- Prioritization of mission problems is essential in finding potential solutions.
- The right team is critical, with people who understand the bureaucracy of DoD as well the commercial world.
- By supporting acquisitions officers to think outside the box, the use of Other Transaction Authorities (OTAs) as contracting authorities was facilitated and the concept for the alternative acquisition authority (CSO) was created.

Querying an agency's workforce, those who see the inner workings of the agency up close each day, about the problems they encounter is an effective way to understand a broad range of agency challenges. It also is an important way to engage the workforce and involve them in the hard work of improving agency delivery of mission impact. Workforce crowdsourcing has long been an effective way to gather input and ideas from across an organization. With the global pandemic we are currently experiencing and the accompanying shift to teleworking and other remote ways of working, workforce crowdsourcing has become a vital way to engage, involve, and retain an increasingly physically distanced organization.

Examples include NASA's NASA@Work effort, which challenges its workforce to deliver creative ideas about the best use of NASA resources, such as how to use unscheduled time on the International Space Station. The GSA 10x program crowdsources across the federal government to identify projects it can build and deliver to federal agencies. And the TSA's TSA@Work, a program running continuously since 2007, finds good ideas from across the workforce and seeks input on the quality of those ideas to prioritize them.

USE CASE 4: National Aeronautics and Space Administration's NASA@WORK
Innovation Problem to Be Solved: *How might NASA better leverage the considerable knowledge and mission focus of its workforce to solve difficult NASA challenges?*

Background: As the growing NASA community matured and the space mission expanded, NASA wanted a way to engage its sizable workforce, which resided in multiple and disconnected centers.

Innovation Solution:
- NASA@Work is an internal, agency-wide platform that provides the NASA community with the ability to provide solutions to agency challenges.
- Open to any NASA employee, contractor, intern, or detailee.
- NASA@Work consists of campaign owners, who craft and post a challenge specific to the NASA mission, and campaign respondents, who submit solutions to the specific problems.
- Campaign challenges are specific, detailed, and focused so respondents can provide short, rapid, and efficient solutions.
- Campaign owners select winners, who receive prizes for contributing the best responses.
- Campaigns are categorized into one of four levels of difficulty, with increasingly valuable prizes awarded for corresponding levels of solutions provided.
- Prizes include personalized astronaut autographs, center tours, screen savers, recognition by center directors, shuttle models, and special twitter account postings.

Lessons Learned:
- Campaigns were refined over time to allow for quick and efficient responses. Early campaigns generated highly complex, long answers, becoming paper exercises, which took a great deal of time to propose as well as to review.
- In response to the growing work-from-home need, NASA@Work expanded its access; the system can be accessed through a publicly available portal using smartcard authentication.

The world of colleges and universities holds a plethora of expertise in a vast number of topics and academic disciplines. Many academic fields not only are highly relevant to federal government work, but also can be essential in driving government advances, for example, engineering insights into military tools, biomedical advancements, mathematical expertise, knowledge of foreign political situations, and computer science inventions. The federal government many decades ago recognized the need to harvest this expertise and to provide researchers and academics the ability to work on some of the most challenging problems, and today there are a substantial number of decades-long relationships between universities and federal agencies. Federal innovation organizations have also recognized the importance of the potentially groundbreaking work ongoing in academia and have devised new ways of accessing this expertise to support federal work.

Two important examples of how innovation organizations have made use of academia include Hacking for Defense (H4D) program, which has expanded beyond DoD support to include other federal agencies, such as the Department of Homeland Security's (DHS) Hacking for Homeland Security, the Department of State's Hacking for Allies, and the National Oceanographic and Atmospheric Administration's Hacking for Oceans, among others. This H4 model enables college and university students, through a semester-long project, to rapidly address difficult emerging agency problems and to deliver proposed solutions back to the sponsoring federal agency.

USE CASE 5: DHS Hacking for Homeland Security (H4HS)
Innovation Problem to be Solved: *How might the DHS leverage the energy and knowledge residing within academia to solve difficult DHS problems?*

Background:
- Although DHS has extensive relationships with its academic Centers of Excellence, they are long-term relationships focused on university efforts, rather than short-term relationships focused on creating solutions for DHS components.
- Developing cross-component solutions was helpful in increasing collaboration and leveraging resources most effectively.
- Although an H4HS program had been considered before, component buy-in to the program meant that students were provided real-world and relevant mission problems to solve.

Innovation Solution: A Hacking for Homeland Security effort, funded by DHS Science and Technology (S&T), modeled on Hacking for Defense, a $1.2M 18-month project focused on providing three universities with hard problems from the Cybersecurity and Infrastructure Security Agency (CISA), the Federal Emergency Management Agency (FEMA), and the Transportation Security Agency (TSA).

Lessons Learned:
- Much was learned from the similar Hacking for Defense program.
- For new programs within the agency, more time is needed to resolve contracting and routinize program processes across multiple components and headquarter organizations.
- Drawing problems from all DHS components, rather than one component agency only, transfers the impact of the program to the entire DHS enterprise.
- The various mission sets across DHS provided a wide range of problems for students to solve, increasing the number of interested students and seeding potential future federal employees.
- The cross-component program allowed for strong collaboration between the agencies and built lasting relationships beyond the program.

Similarly, the National Science Foundation's (NSF) iCorps program supports exploration within federal agencies of the entrepreneurial process. iCorps training integrates the scientific method of inquiry and industrial discovery in a data-driven culture characterized by rigor, relevance, and evidence, resulting in researchers translating a promising idea from the lab to potential commercial use. The President Innovation Fellows (PIF) program is another means for the federal government to leverage expertise residing outside government personnel; it awards year-long fellowships to highly qualified experts with exceptional resumes. PIFs are typically mid- and senior-level experts in data, artificial intelligence, engineering, product design and user experience, and digital strategy who are deployed across federal agencies to assist with solving difficult problems using their specific knowledge to support existing agency resources.

PRIZES & CHALLENGES

The federal government has the ability to fund and run "prize and challenge" efforts, in which external talent can solve a specific problem in exchange for a prize, usually money. Congressionally provided laws give authority for running such events to specific federal agencies, which can benefit from drawing on external expertise, usually in the computer science, engineering, or technical arenas. However, most federal agencies, in order to make use of these creative ways to leverage external expertise, have the ability to partner with the federally mandated agencies with prize and challenge authority.

Prize and challenge initiatives focus attention and effort on specific problems; they originated with mathematician David Hilbert, who over a century ago defined a set of unsolved problems to spark interest in the field of mathematics and progress on solving the problems. The General Services Administration (GSA) hosts the federal Challenge and Prize Community of Practice with over 1,000 government personnel running a wide range of competitions that seek solutions to difficult agency problems, usually from individuals or teams outside of the agency, such as from academia or the private sector.

The range of prizes and challenges includes hackathons, data jams, grand challenges, and mapathons—all are efforts that use crowdsourcing to gather solutions that have a mission impact. One particular subset of prizes and challenges is the "shark tank" competition, based on the television show of the same name that began airing in 2009. Since then, federal agencies have adopted a similar format of problem solvers pitching their innovative ideas to a panel of judges to vie for a prize, which may be further funding or support for the idea and resulting solution. Federal shark tank competitions have blossomed, including the AFWERX Spark Tank competition, an annual event at which airmen pitch innovation ideas to solve operational problems.

MAKERS

The maker community, initially an outgrowth of a hardware approach within the hacking communities, focuses on making new tools, technologies, and prototypes by providing "makers" materials in which to build the tools from existing or wholly new items, to include electronics, coding, 3-D printing, or metalworking. Makers are a unique resource within the federal government, as the efforts can be more costly to operate and can be less flexible in pivoting to meet changing mission requirements.

One of the best-known and well-respected maker efforts is Kessel Run, the operational name for the U.S. Air Force Life Cycle Management Center's (AFLCMC) Detachment 12. Kessel Run builds, tests, delivers, operates, and maintains cloud-based infrastructure and warfighting software applications for operations around the world. The speed and effectiveness of Kessel Run rivals commercial capabilities and is a model for quickly creating and deploying mission-focused tools.

Other examples of makers include the National Aeronautics and Space Administration's (NASA) Space Shop at the Ames Research Center, which provides any employee access to a full range of tools, machine shop, and electronic equipment to work on projects of their choosing, as well as technical support for them to use the tools. The U.S. Navy's NavalX has a similar maker facility at its headquarters. The Immigration and Customs Enforcement HSI Innovation Lab is the agency's centralized hub for developing analytics capabilities, tools, and enhanced business processes.

FACILITATORS

Facilitators across the federal government are increasingly utilizing the common innovation methods innovation, to include design thinking, human-centered design, acceleration, storytelling, and other methods in their work. By increasing the skillsets of federal facilitators, they can better serve the needs of project, problem, or mission-focused teams in developing strategies, communication, collaboration, team building and solutions. Project AGITARE is a community of federal facilitators, funded by the nonprofit organization, Defense Entrepreneurs Forum (DEF), which provides extensive resources, tools, and training for both facilitators and teams that need facilitation.

Note that the work of facilitators does not fit well into the Innovation Pipeline model but is still worth mentioning in describing the major types of federal innovators, given facilitators' focus and use of core innovation methodologies.

3.3 Understanding Startup Culture

It is difficult to avoid the drumbeat of the rapid pace of innovation in new technologies—including those in the fields of cybersecurity tools, artificial intelligence, autonomy, access to space, drones, 5G, biotechnology, quantum, microelectronics— that were once owned and developed by the U.S. government but are no longer being led by the military or government labs. These tools now come from commercial vendors, many of them China-based companies, which prevents their purchase by the U.S. government. DoD no longer controls, nor can it predict, what future technologies will be developed.

Our national security is now inexorably intertwined with cutting-edge commercial technology and is hindered by the government's inability to quickly acquire, transition, and utilize that technology. Therefore, its critical to understand how startups, temporary organizations designed to search for a repeatable and scalable business model in order to become a company, think and operate, given that they are the likely source of emerging technology. And understanding the culture of startup organizations gives insight into how we can leverage the best of startup culture to benefit government innovation.

There are fundamental cultural differences in the commercial startup world compared to the federal government. But, essentially, your government innovation effort is a startup—you face many of the same challenges (for example, questioning of your choices and tactics) and constraints (for example, resources and time). A startup can serve as an important model to emulate and replicate, possibly improving the way in which the federal government acts and performs.

It is estimated that 90% of startups fail, a staggeringly high percentage. Why such a high percentage of commercial failure? According to a recent industry survey, the primary cause is lack of market demand. Customers are not willing to pay for products or services that don't meet their needs. And in industry, the only measure of success for a product is that customers are willing to pay for it; effort and energy count for nothing unless a product will sell.

Imagine if 90% of government projects failed. In fact, there is almost no tolerance for any failure in government projects and programs, given that taxpayer dollars fund federal efforts. The analogy between startups and government organizations is obvious; the only efforts that matter are those with true mission impact. We must therefore assiduously and constantly assess the ability to create mission impact with our solutions. Using metrics to measure not only the innovation actions undertaken, but also, more importantly, the mission impact, is critical (for further input, see Module 8).

Other reasons for lack of startup success include insufficient financial resources, putting together the wrong team, failing to be first to market or best in market (not serving customer needs,) pricing and cost issues, lack of passion and innovation, and lack of a business model— all reasons that can also explain the failure of government projects and programs. It becomes apparent, as we learn more about the peculiarities of startup culture, that many lessons from world of startups can inform and improve the way in which government innovation can thrive.

"Fail fast" is a startup maxim, meaning that failure in business is inevitable, even desirable, as long as you quickly act to fix the flawed concept. Government, too, can benefit from learning the appropriate lessons from failure quickly and applying those lessons learned to the next experiment. It is not only the challenges we face with rapid acquisition that prevents the government from moving with speed; U.S. federal laws and government policies can also hinder our ability to move quickly to solutions. Being a "fast follower" and learning quickly therefore is critical to increasing the speed with which we can achieve finding and transitioning the right solutions to our problems.

Central to startup culture is the notion that we should never expect to initially have the right solution. We must try multiple solutions; learning along the way what does and doesn't work, especially learning with each attempt what customers need and want, is the recipe for increasing success. Rapidly gathering input from customers along the way to to be able to modify the product to better meet customer wants and needs is the goal.

It is worth noting that industry startups, as well as serving as a model worth emulating, can also be important sources of emerging technologies for government use, provided that the acquisition authority and process can be adequately managed.

Module 3 Key Takeaways

- There are over 300 federal innovation efforts, using many different models of organization; your agency's innovation efforts should strategically address agency opportunities.

- Federal innovation efforts fall into several major categories: commercial technology acquisition; workforce crowdsourcing; leveraging academia and research; prizes and challenges; makers and facilitators.

- With government organizations, the only efforts that matter are those with mission impact

- Failure in business is inevitable, even desirable.

- Treat government innovation solutions like commercial tools: only create solutions that your "customers will buy."

- Testing multiple solutions increases the chance of having the right solution.

EXERCISE: CREATING YOUR INNOVATION MODEL

This exercise will help you better understand your agency's strengths, weaknesses, opportunities, and threats (SWOT), and how an innovation approach can address them. If you already have an innovation organization, how might this knowledge help shape it's goals and approach?

What are your agency's strengths?

1 _____

2 _____

3 _____

What are your agency's weaknesses?

1 _____

2 _____

3 _____

What are your agency's opportunities?

1 _____

2 _____

3 _____

What are threats to your agency?

1 _____

2 _____

3 _____

Which specific factor within the above SWOT categories is most pressing in fulfilling your agency's mission?

_____

_____

_____

Which factor is currently unaddressed in fulfilling your agency's mission?

_____

_____

_____

Which factor could be addressed by creating external partnerships?

_____

_____

_____

How could you leverage an agency strength to address a critical weakness or threat?

_____

_____

_____

How could you leverage an agency opportunity to address a central weakness or threat?

_____

_____

_____

What innovation model can best address your agency's SWOT categories? Will an internal or external solution be most effective? Build upon ideas created in the Module 2 and 3 exercises.

_____

_____

_____

_____

_____

Notes:

BUILDING INNOVATION ORGANIZATIONS

4.1 Introduction

In building your innovation organization or in supporting innovation across your agency, certain building blocks are essential to creating an effective and robust effort and ensure that you have the required expertise, insights, and experience to be successful. The quality of the people, resources, and ideas you leverage in your innovation efforts will determine your ability to create impactful mission outcomes that demonstrate to your colleagues and leadership how innovation can make a difference in your agency. In this module, we focus on building the operational support you need to fully bring your Innovation Pipeline to life.

Innovation and innovative organizations, whether in the commercial or public sector, have common characteristics they share that help them be more innovative, including:

- A focus on the end user and mission demands (or the customer and market, in commercial industry)
- A focus on speed, whether of invention, creation, adoption, adaptation, or deployment
- Tolerance for risk-taking
- An ability to pivot when required

And you, as either the lead program manager or key actor in creating innovation, can play a critical role in embodying and instilling these characteristics throughout the entire Innovation Pipeline process.

4.2 Key Components of Innovative Organizations

The following components are foundational to innovation efforts and should be considered when crafting your innovation approach.

PEOPLE

Nothing happens in government without people. They drive actions at every level of the organization. Leverage the greatest possible number of people to assist you in creating innovation, with the goal of engaging your entire agency workforce in the project to expand the impact of innovation across the agency.

Include all who want to be part of your innovation efforts to build interest in and advocacy for innovation across and beyond your agency, but understand the difference between interested allies and those with the power to make decisions or affect resources. Those who are advocates can generate interest in others and serve as messengers about your project, program, and innovation efforts. Those with power can affect your efforts both positively and negatively; work with this group to find common goals and show that innovation can help them achieve these goals more effectively.

Additionally, agency leaders can be excellent sources of innovation within their own organizations and can contribute to helping the agency embrace innovation. They can also be sources of problems, however; when you begin and continue the relationship-building discussions, you will hear their pain points concerning agency processes, goals, strategies, and actions, which may illuminate problems and give ideas for potential solutions, but may also be outside the scope of your efforts or not align with agency mission.

Two specific groups to focus on when building your innovation efforts are senior support and your innovation team.

Senior leader refers to the executive champion of the innovation effort and the central stakeholder. This person's impact on innovation success cannot be overestimated. The priorities of senior leadership are resourced and supported across their agency and garner attention at every level in the organization. The senior leader may not be the person to whom you directly report but can ensure that innovation is prioritized when determining resourcing and priorities. This support, and hopefully the ear of the senior leader, ensures tight coordination on innovation activities, insight into agency priorities that can align with innovation efforts, adequate resourcing, and the ability to modify innovation efforts to respond to changing leadership priorities.

To build your **Innovation team** (with either direct-line or dotted-line responsibility) and associated personnel (perhaps detailees, reservists, rotational staff, or contractors), select those who embody the innovation characteristics highlighted above. By doing so, you will be able to move your innovation efforts forward more easily. If you are an innovation team member, either directly or indirectly, strive to exemplify the characteristics of speed, user focus, risk-taking, and ability to pivot in all of your innovation support. Seriously consider each team member and their area of expertise to ensure you have the appropriate team assembled to execute your mission. Identify any areas in which you are missing specific skill sets, knowledge, or experience to target and recruit the right mix of personnel.

PARTNERSHIPS

Partnerships can be created with anyone outside your innovation organization, your agency, or the federal government who can provide opportunities to expand and deliver on your innovation or pipeline goals. Partnerships serve as a force multiplier for your innovation efforts, expanding the resource you have to execute your mission far beyond your existing capacity, and increasing your agency's ability to more effectively meet its mission by using the resources of other agencies.

Partners can include virtually anyone and any organization—other federal agencies, allied and foreign partners or international companies, nonprofits, academia, industry, and state and local agencies. Partnerships can be created through formal means, such as Partnership Intermediary Agreements (PIAs), Memoranda of Agreement (MOAs), or Memorandum of Understanding (MOUs), perhaps by signing nondisclosure agreements (NDAs). They can be loosely formed via informal means, such as public-private partnerships, such as Dcode and the National Security Innovation Network (NSIN). Partnerships can even be created through a series of emails and a handshake.

Other agency, component, and federal innovation staff can suggest partnership opportunities you may not have been aware of that could assist you in finding solutions for your innovation problems or in identifying projects that could build your innovation programs. Potential partners may have existing acquisition vehicles, with sufficient room on the contract to fund your projects. They may even be looking for partners to work on a collaborative project with your specific mission focus.

Look for enabling partnerships within your agency that can help with our innovation projects or missions. Potential partnerships can include offices of science and technology (S&T) that may be looking for partners or program managers to drive new efforts, financial officers with a strong understanding of how resources are allocated across your agency and who support rapid acquisition methods, management offices that may be invested in finding more innovative ways to do their business, or even a chief innovation officer who seeks ways to drive innovation across your organization.

In building your network beyond your stakeholders, it's important to have friends everywhere; you never know what opportunities you may stumble across or how a relationship can blossom into a partnership. With each new person you meet, assume that multiple opportunities exist to partner with them. By asking questions and asserting your innovation needs, you can elicit the ways in which you can partner effectively.

Examples of innovative federal partnerships are numerous and instructive in highlighting how partnerships can achieve mission impact. In-Q-Tel, originally the Central Intelligence Agency's venture capital arm to identify, fund, and transition early-stage commercial technologies into the agency, has expanded to include the broader intelligence community, DoD, DHS, and the broader federal government. Other examples include the DEFENSEWERX constellation and its eight innovation hubs, including the DoD's Special Operations Command SOFWERX and the U.S. Army Cyber Command Cyber Fusion Innovation Center, and the General Services Administration's 18F program, which builds and buys technology on behalf of its federal partners.

Use Case 6: SOFWERX

Innovation Problem to Be Solved: *How might SOCOM solve challenging warfighter problems quickly by prototyping solutions and creating strategies, collaboration, and events to enable these solutions?*

Background:
- Since inception, the U.S. Army's Special Operations Command (SOCOM) has been legendary in creating innovative tools and using ingenuity to assist its special operations.
- An incredibly proficient organization in solving its problems through innovation, SOCOM drew from primarily internal capabilities.

Innovation Solution:
- SOFWERX was created to "reinvent how SOCOM invents," by utilizing a much wider set of interagency partners, including industry and academia, to promote divergent thought to solve difficult problems for Special Forces units.
- SOFWERX, the first of now eight DEFENSEWERX innovation hubs, was created via a Partnership Intermediary Agreement (PIA) between DEFENSEWERX and the U.S. Special Operations Command (USSOCOM) as a groundbreaking federal innovation effort.
- It utilizes flexible acquisition methodologies to purchase commercial technologies quickly.
- SOFWERX held a number of successful collaborative projects and events, such as ThunderDrone, which focused on rapid prototyping of commercial drone technologies for land, sea, and air for the Special Ops community. The Game of Drones competition provided $600,000 in cash prizes for successful demonstrations of counter unmanned aerial systems.

Lessons Learned:
- By bringing together a wide range of interagency partners, SOFWERX increased the chances that innovative solutions could be found and utilized to benefit SOCOM.
- Building a vast number of relationships increased the opportunity to solve the right problem at the right time by the right people. Not all relationships might be known as to how they would prove useful, but building the relationship set conditions for future success.
- By using an "abundance mindset" vs a scarcity mindset, SOFWERX recognized that many innovative solutions already existed in the commercial sector but needed to be more quickly identified and leveraged.[3]

CONTRACTING AUTHORITIES AND ACQUISITION

Some of you are more than familiar with the impressive beast that is the DoD's Acquisition Life Cycle Management framework, how the DoD purchases a significant portion of its tools. This incredibly complex process can consume a career in mastering the processes and expertise required to negotiate it. Other federal agencies have somewhat less complex but nonetheless challenging acquisition processes. For very good reasons, there is a system of checks and balances when spending taxpayer dollars for mission benefit; the level of responsibility in being good stewards of this funding is immense. Yet the byzantine and enormously complex and slow process means that most cutting-edge emerging commercial technologies cannot be purchased, limiting the resources that can be leveraged and shutting out many smaller commercial technologies.

---

[3]Weiss, Mitchell, *We the Possibility: Harnessing Public Entrepreneurship to Solve Our Most Urgent Problems.* (Cambridge, MA: Harvard Business Review Press.), pg. 33.

FIGURE 4.1 THE BEAST THAT IS DEFENSE ACQUISITION

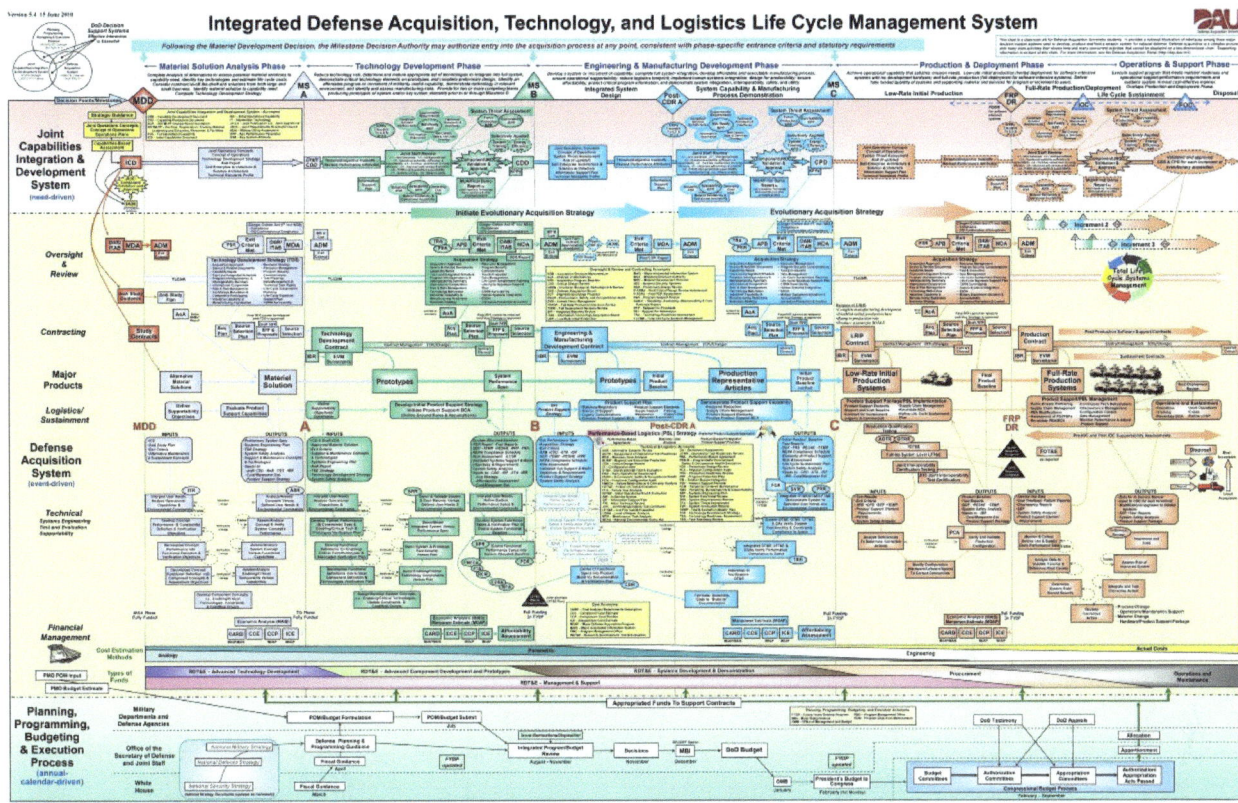

Standard federal acquisition processes clash with innovation goals of speed and risk-taking. One major goal in acquisition processes is to remove or minimize the risk of purchasing using government funds, but in building this necessary risk protection, speed is sacrificed because of the amount of paperwork required and the number of steps or people involved in the acquisition process. Standard acquisition processes also may hinder effective communication between government and industry technical experts in articulating requirements or in discussing constraints and advantages of possible solutions.

Federal acquisition processes exist to clarify the mission need, to establish the requirements in filling the mission need, to reduce the level of risk, primarily for the federal government but also for the commercial entity, to outline the requirements for solution development and production, and to describe sustainment before the project is undertaken and funded. Regulation of federal acquisition is necessary to ensure diminished risk, to ensure competition, to award contracts with the best value, and to prevent waste, fraud, and abuse or any potential conflicts of interest. Finally,

acquisition processes manage both federal and contractor behaviors to achieve these goals.

It will serve you well to know your agency's contracting authorities, the acquisition experts and leadership, and to map the processes so that you fully understand the requirements, the people involved in the process, and the time line required for each step. By mastering these details, you are best suited to help re-engineer them in collaboration with your acquisition stakeholders to better meet your particular innovation needs. Find out which other agencies have contracting authorities and even contracting vehicles you can join, which can often speed up the acquisition process. Form relationships with your contracting colleagues and emphasize your desire to work collaboratively to achieve common goals.

Within the innovation realm, acquisition is all about speed: using and applying authorities in a way that creates rapid innovation, especially in acquiring commercial technologies. Generally, using alternative or rapid acquisition authorities will speed the acquisition process.

Over the last two decades, there has been an increasing desire to change how the federal government purchases commercial capabilities, resulting in the creation of several new and more flexible acquisition authorities. These authorities, which include both Federal Acquisition Regulation (FAR) and non-FAR-based authorities (shown in Figure 4.3), include the Small Business Innovation Research and Small Business Technology Transfer programs, Other Transaction Authorities (OTAs), and research and development agreements (R&D) agreements, such as Partnership Intermediary Agreements (PIAs). There are resources supporting the use of the alternative authorities, including the Defense Acquisition University (DAU), which provides extensive training and online tools, and offices such as the DHS Procurement Innovation Lab (PIL), which partners with DHS organizations and individuals to support alternative contracting methods and help navigate acquisition hurdles more easily.

There are a number of reasons why utilizing alternative authorities can be advantageous. They can speed acquisition and procurement, sometimes quite significantly, and they may require less paperwork to establish. These authorities are created by Congress and so, by definition, do not circumvent laws and policies. These authorities and the processes to establish them are becoming increasingly well-known and understood across the federal government, making the use of them more common. And it is possible to lower administrative costs by streamlining the processes to establish them.

But there are also challenges to using alternative acquisition methods. Contracting officers build entire careers around understanding the nuances of government purchasing and acquisition, undergoing years of training to be careful, methodical, detailed, and thorough in their work; the responsibility of wisely spending taxpayer dollars is enormous, with grave penalties for doing so irresponsibly. However, these behaviors that ensure the federal government has created a legion of acquisition professionals are antithetical to those that ensure success in using commercial technologies: speed in identifying and obtaining trailblazing technologies to solve mission challenges, flexibility in finding creative ways of hastening government purchasing, and comfort with trying new methods to achieve the desired pace and accepting the risk that comes with trying new processes.

FIGURE 4.2. THE DEFENSE ACQUISITION UNIVERSITY (DAU) ACQUISITION AUTHORITIES FAN

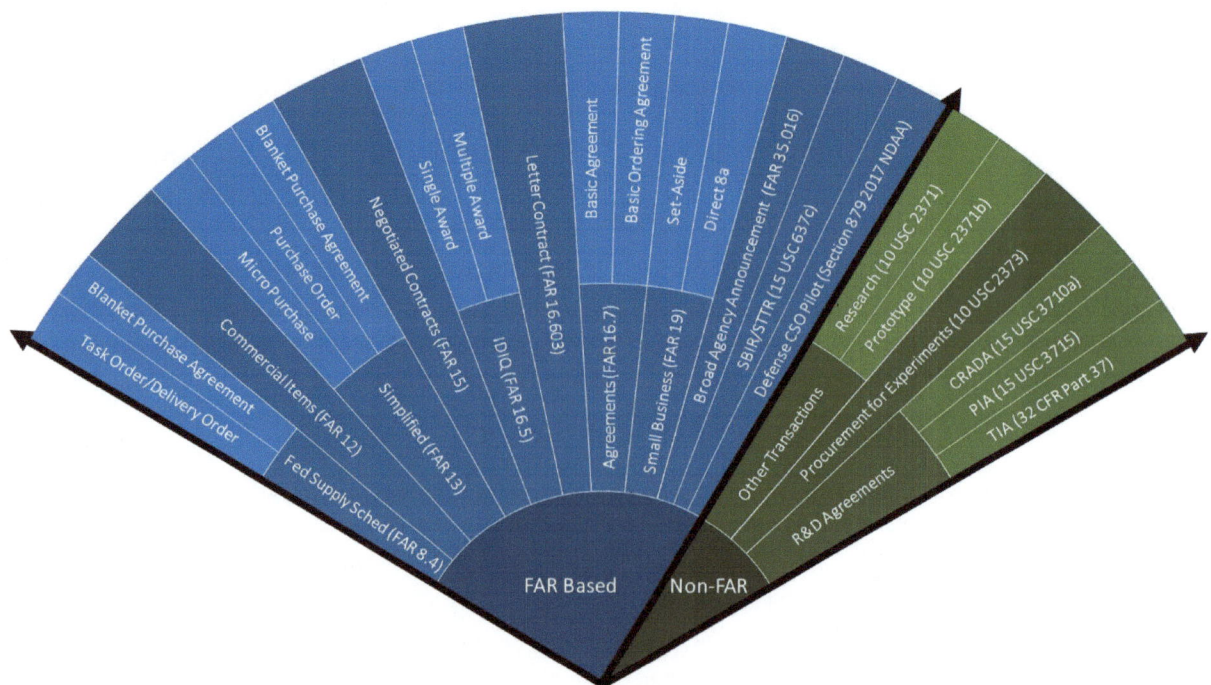

Given the complexity of federal acquisition processes, using alternative acquisition methods may feel like a risky venture to contracting officers, who may not know or feel comfortable with using alternative or new authorities to make purchases due to lack of knowledge or familiarity with their processes. The penalties for error are great; some may feel that the benefit of trying new methods that may or may not provide advantages over more traditional methods is not worth the risk. And we all know that implementing any new process is inherently painful. For many, it is simply easier and less risky to stick with tried-and-true methodologies to do our daily work.

Understanding your agency's existing authorities is the first step to using them most effectively, and working closely with a trust acquisition partner is key. Look for a partner who is comfortable with and excited by thinking outside of the box—and who is looking for a program partner to help them try some interesting new ways of working. No doubt your agency has a number of authorities provided to it that aren't being utilized fully or with aspects that are not currently being maximized. Understand which agencies have other authorities not currently provided to your agency and how you might be able to leverage those authorities, working collaboratively with that agency. Work closely with your legal partner to understand the nuances of how to exploit the full authority and how to partner most effectively with the agency. Your last resort is advocating for a new authority to be created within Congress, but obviously this is a long shot fraught with challenges.

You can also partner with your acquisition colleagues to help them leverage resources to learn more about OTAs and alternative acquisition processes. The DAU provides excellent training on alternative authorities and processes; other federal agencies provide similar training. Your agency's Office of the Chief Financial Officer may be able to share their expertise on alternative authorities and processes and train other acquisition colleagues. Or your agency may have offices you can leverage, such as DHS's PIL, which provides training and education to help make purchasing an easier and faster process.

Again, as an innovation leader focused on bringing change to your agency's culture, you can help shift the thinking about acquisition, although you may require the assistance of leadership across your agency to realize this change.

FUNDING

Regardless of the approach taken to achieve innovation within your organization (discussed further in Module 4) and like with any government effort, resources are essential to getting work accomplished, including billets for personnel and purchase of contracting support and programmatic activities. Only so much can be accomplished by one individual acting alone. If your innovation efforts are not funded, they are likely to quickly devolve into innovation theater. And regardless of the growth and expansion of innovation efforts, becoming a program of record as quickly as possible with dedicated funding and personnel should be your goal.

There are several ways in which dedicated funding can be realized:

- Perhaps innovation is already a program of record within your organization and has dedicated funding and personnel to execute and sustain innovation efforts—congratulations! Now it is essential to show continual return on that agency investment by illustrating how your innovation efforts achieve agency strategies and leadership priorities. For more information on tracking and communicating the successes of your program, see Module 8.
- Your senior sponsor and/or agency leadership may have prioritized innovation and mandated use of discretionary CIO funding on an annual basis. Although this is a good way to start and build an innovation effort, it is too dependent on leadership predilection; leadership preferences could change or leadership may be replaced. Identify those leaders who are responsible for creating programs of record within your agency and focus on becoming a program of record. Articulate your mission impact regularly using metrics to illustrate your successes.
- Allocation of programmatic dollars from existing programs, per leadership mandate

with one or more resource sponsors, is another way to aggregate resources for your efforts. This approach may not win you any friends within the existing programs, who may resent having to reallocate some of their funding. Work closely with program managers to ensure that you understand and simultaneously meet their goals with your innovation efforts. See Module 5 for further guidance.

- Congressional support for innovation efforts within your agency can be a way to sustain your program each year, if congressional authorizers designate and appropriators execute a "mark" within your agency's funding bill to ensure that agency innovation efforts are legislatively and financially supported. Innovation is popular these days with federal leadership and in Congress. However, seeking congressional attention is both risky and difficult, and requires leadership support, assistance from your legislative office, and possible external advocacy on the Hill. Congressional support should not be counted on to sustain your program each year, given the vagaries of congressional funding.

Each of these ways to receive funding for innovation efforts clearly requires the good will, advocacy, and support from a variety of individuals within your organization, including your leadership, senior sponsor, and the CIO. Their advocacy will be best supported by real data illustrating that your innovation efforts result in mission impact for the agency.

What if you don't have funding for your innovation efforts? Often in government, nascent projects based on good ideas are provided few or no needed resources, whether they are personnel or billets to be filled, detailees from other offices and programs, or one-year programmatic dollars with carte blanche from the Chief Financial Officer per the Senior Official's decree. Often, leadership will first try to determine whether an idea will create a groundswell within an organization, capture the attention of other key players within the organization, and start to make good things happen without any resources being allocated. Or

leadership might envision innovation permeating an organization, rather than residing in one office, or emphasize the type of innovation, such as workforce engagement, that doesn't require the purchase and transition of technology. If so, the clock is ticking on making good things happen with innovation across your organization. Work hard to achieve mission successes, communicate them regularly, and continue to focus on becoming a program of record.

For innovation efforts focused on commercial technology acquisition, the "color of money," or type of funding you receive, is critical to how you can best execute these dollars. If you do not have significant acquisition or government purchasing experience, ensure you have dedicated acquisition expertise on your team so you can execute these dollars quickly and effectively to meet mission needs. The type of funding created to support federal efforts has changed over time, with research dollars staying flat and operational system development increasing significantly in the last 20 years. Develop relationships within the CIO shop to understand how to best influence the type of money you can execute.

Title IV RDT&E Funding by Character of Work, FY1996-FY2020

obligational authority, in billions of current dollars

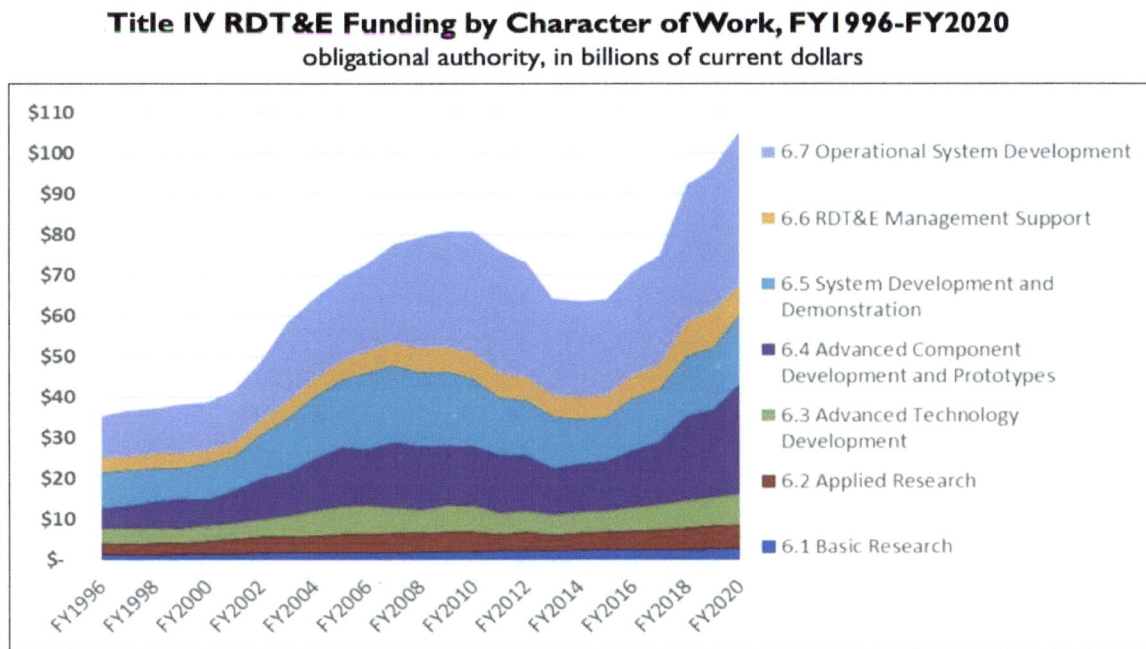

SOURCE: CRS ANALYSIS OF DATA FROM DEPARTMENT OF DEFENSE, RESEARCH, DEVELOPMENT, TEST, AND EVALUATION PROGRAMS (R-1) FOR FY1998-FY2021.

AGENCY SUPPORT

Within each agency, office-level support can provide the resources your innovation efforts require to adequately address the range of challenges you will face. The following are some of the offices that you should plan to engage with to garner their support.

Legal: An important first step in bringing innovation to life is ensuring that legal counsel, from the beginning of your innovation efforts, understands your goals and leadership support for innovation. Offices of General Counsel will want to be included in your thinking, your activities, and your partnerships and can either make or break these efforts, depending on how they see them in relation to their philosophy. Legal counsel can be an enormous ally and advocate across the agency for innovation, or they can stymie your efforts at every turn. Is your legal team trying to bring new ways of doing things to the agency? Are they trying to "get to yes"? If so, find an ally, as senior as possible, within the office early and bring them into your vision. Find mutual goals and show how you can help them in achieving these goals. Are they more traditional thinkers, not inclined to view new ways of doing business as important? If so, understand their goals, their motivations, their pain points, and their needs and then work on achieving

their goals and your goals simultaneously, setting the expectation that together, you will get to "yes."

At the end of the day, legal counsel are advisors, not deciders; help them be that advisor. Having a coordinated and collaborative relationship with your legal counsel with a deep and mutual understanding can save you and your team tremendous amounts of time, energy, and frustration down the road.

Security: As with your legal office, early situational awareness and understanding of your innovation goals and projects within security will save you a great deal of time as begin to incubate and transition commercial technologies into your agency or as you negotiate partnership agreements and contracts with external partners.

Office of the Chief Information Officer (IT): The OCIO will be vital to your success, especially if any of your innovation projects require that commercial technologies be brought into the agency. Engage with them early to inform them about your goals and find mutual goals for collaboration.

Testing and Development: Your agency may have an office responsible for ensuring the proper development of tools by fielding them with end users to ensure their efficacy, safety, and readiness for deployment. Working closely with this office can be critical in leveraging existing agency resources early in the process.

Strategy and Policy: This office should be a natural partner to innovation efforts, given the importance of innovation across the federal government. They can help you craft foundational documents to establish your office and set precedents for driving innovation throughout the agency.

Human Resources: With leadership and program manager support, HR can assist with driving innovation across the agency by building innovation performance goals into individual annual performance plans.

Congressional Liaison: Simply put, if Congress doesn't support you, you won't survive long-term as a program of record. With "the power of the purse," Congress is able to inject resources into your effort or redirect funding from your program to another they find of more utility in delivering agency mission impact.

METRICS

Creating ways to measure the effectiveness and efficiency of your Innovation Pipeline is essential to ensure success in meeting mission priorities and achieving mission impact. Metrics inform your senior leadership and sponsor about

program performance, progress, and activities and alert them to your innovation and mission successes. Tracking metrics can apprise your action officers of steps and activities within the pipeline that need increased attention and how to adjust the pipeline to maximize its efficiency and effectiveness in delivering mission impact. And metrics can illustrate with real and measurable data where additional resources are needed to increase productivity within specific steps of the pipeline. For further information on how to measure your Innovation Pipeline, see Module 8.

COMMUNICATIONS

Communication is fundamental to creating buy-in and awareness at all levels of your organization. Communicate frequently to leadership, to stakeholders and executors of the work, and to beneficiaries and end users of the problems, projects, and program so they are informed about your vision, the progress being made in achieving the vision, the roadblocks you are experiencing, and the successes achieved. Communicating to stakeholders your common goals and interests will go a long way toward creating allies among them.

4.3 Building an Operational Support Plan

By including each of these elements in your plan for your Innovation Pipeline, you will significantly reduce the risk of your solutions, projects, and even your innovation program facing insurmountable challenges or potentially existential threats. Again, not every organization has the resources to formally devote every element mentioned here to your innovation efforts. Sometimes even an informal advisor from one of these key support roles (for example, legal, legislative, or acquisition) will be enough of a resource to ensure you are heading in the right direction, connecting with the right experts, and using the appropriate tools.

Use the exercises in this module to build out your plan. Refer to Appendices A and B to gain further insight into the types of skill sets needed for your pipeline.

Module 4 Key Takeaways

- Core tenets of innovation include laser focus on the end user, working at speed, tolerating risk, and pivoting quickly.

- Senior support for innovation efforts is critical to success.

- Partnerships greatly expand the finite resources available to create mission impact through innovation.

- Using alternative acquisition authorities and OTAs and working collaboratively with acquisition professionals may make acquisition faster and easier.

- Frequent and regular communication regarding innovation vision, goals, projects, and successes at every level of your agency creates a common understanding.

EXERCISE: RESOURCING YOUR INNOVATION PIPELINE

This exercise will help you develop the key components of innovation organizations for your Innovation Pipeline (number of personnel/detailees/ contractors; stakeholders; partners; contracting authorities; funding; legal support; security; senior support; congressional support).

Personnel and areas of expertise

1 _____

2 _____

3 _____

4 _____

5 _____

Partners

1 _____

2 _____

3 _____

4 _____

5 _____

Existing acquisition authorities; any additional authorities needed?

1 _____

2 _____

3 _____

4 _____

5 _____

Funding

_____

_____

_____

Agency support (legal, security, CIO, testing and development, strategy, HR, legislative)

1 _____

2 _____

3 _____

4 _____

5 _____

What communication methods should I use and to whom do I need to communicate regularly?

1 _____

2 _____

3 _____

4 _____

5 _____

EXERCISE: MAPPING YOUR AGENCY'S ACQUISITION PROCESS

This exercise will help you map your agency's acquisition process, key players, and key deliverables. Map the process below, highlighting key players in each step and the outcomes for each. Collaborating with your colleagues is encouraged!

EXISTING AUTHORITIES

1

2

3

4

5

PARTNER AUTHORITIES

1

2

3

VEHICLES

1

2

3

BUILDING YOUR STAKEHOLDER NETWORK

5.1 Introduction

Stakeholders are the individuals and organizations who have a vested interest in your activities. One of your most important jobs in driving innovation efforts within your agency is determining who your stakeholders are and understanding their needs, motivations, priorities, and challenges and how your innovation efforts align with their sense of how the agency can best achieve its mission. Being a master of networks is fundamental to innovation success and mission impact through innovation by leveraging stakeholder networks and building strong relationships with them. This is a continuing process requiring constant attention, as frequent government personnel changes, not to mention military and intelligence community rotations, mean that your stakeholder networks will constantly be changing.

5.2 Leveraging Stakeholders to Drive Innovation

Working effectively with your stakeholders can create buy-in and support from the widest network possible. Sharing your vision, goals, objectives, successes, and future plans will help them understand what your innovation efforts are about. You should routinely and intentionally assess your stakeholders, allies, and advocates and how their interests are aligning with or differing from your own. Having allies—those who support you—is good; however, having advocates—those who proactively drive your interests in ways that influence resourcing—is even better. Communicating to your stakeholders the commonalities between your goals and interests and finding opportunities to succeed together will go a long way toward creating allies and advocates among them.

By building and working a stakeholder network, you are creating messengers at many levels both within and outside your organization, all who can serve as a proxy for you in discussions and environments you aren't part of. When your stakeholders are advocates and know your goals and activities, they can serve as a force multiplier to drive your agenda. Constantly seek to identify new stakeholders and potential partners, and include all those who want to be part of your innovation efforts. You may not always initially know how they can best serve your greater purposes, but the connections will serve you well in the months and years to follow, as you expand and grow your efforts into new areas of mission impact.

Stakeholders fall into several categories: those with interest in innovation, those with power, those with both, and those with neither. Interested stakeholders are important in driving attention to your project and in creating interest among others; those stakeholders will be allies. Stakeholders with power can make decisions about resources and funding, to your benefit or to your detriment; they have the potential to be advocates. By knowing how to categorize each stakeholder, you can more easily discern what can be asked or expected of them and how to best approach them.

Build empathy and create powerful connections with your stakeholders by telling compelling stories about your and your team's efforts and the mission impacts you've made, allowing them to picture their and their teams' role in your vision, creating shared goals for success. Whenever possible, it is important to craft your story based on an understanding of their interests, so you can create mutually beneficial goals and plans. Stakeholders who can share your story in their own words are powerful emissaries.

Work to build an extensive network not only of government contacts, including military and intelligence, but also of industry and academic experts. Build networks around specific problem areas; around ideas, information, opportunities, and existing solutions (and their limitations); around end users with problems; and around potential solution owners. Note that this "sourcing fusion cell" can also include sourcing contacts, potential technologies, capabilities, industry contacts, and companies.

There are a number of cross-agency federal innovation groups that bring together innovation-focused colleagues to share best practices and lessons learned, as well as to showcase recent successes and methodologies. These groups include the Federal Innovation Salon, the Federal Innovation Council, and the Defense Entrepreneurs Forum, as well as some agency-focused groups, like the DHS Innovation Collaborative. Participating in the groups provides an additional way to build networks and learn of innovation opportunities other agencies have successfully utilized.

5.3 Key Stakeholders to Drive Innovation

There are some obvious choices of key stakeholders who can significantly impact your success. In creating your innovation team, consider the following critical stakeholders.

- **Senior Leader:** Previously highlighted in Module 4 as the executive champion of the innovation effort and the central stakeholder. The impact of this person to innovation success cannot overestimated. Having the ear and hopefully the support of the senior leader ensures coordination on innovation activities, insight into agency priorities that can align with innovation efforts, adequate resourcing, and the ability to modify innovation efforts to respond to changing leadership priorities.

- **Beneficiaries and Users:** Those who will ultimately use the innovation solution or benefit from the innovation effort. Intimately understanding their needs, pain points, and desires is critical to crafting solutions that effectively address real mission issues. This group is analogous to commercial sector customers, who drive the creation of products—and the termination of them as well.

- **Action Officers:** Innovation team members (either through direct-line or dotted-line responsibility) who are responsible for executing the daily actions associated with creating, driving, and monitoring the Innovation Pipeline's activities and assessment.

- **Technical Experts:** Those with specific technical skill sets; they may be acquisition, contracting, or financial officers; engineers; coders; policy experts; human resources or security officers; or communications and public affairs officers. Whenever possible, draw upon the problem owners or those closest to the problems you are facing; they are best suited to identify appropriate stakeholders and thus can be most effective.

- **Key Partners:** Collaborators, whether internal or external to your agency, who can assist you in achieving mutually beneficial innovation goals. Partners have ongoing, near-term, or future projects that you can leverage or join. They may be formidable allies who can solve problems for you both, or they may have existing contracting authorities or vehicles you can use. By working closely with key partners, building strong relationships, understanding their existing projects, and learning from their successes and failures, you can leverage their funds and expertise to benefit your own innovation efforts.

USE CASE 7: U.S. Agency for International Development's (USAID) Global Innovation Exchange (GIE)
Innovation Problem to Be Solved: *How might USAID, given its mission (support America's foreign policy, lead USG international development and disaster assistance through partnerships and investments that save lives, reduce poverty, strengthen democratic governance, and help people emerge from humanitarian crises and progress beyond assistance), leverage the skills and knowledge of the entire globe to solve difficult, high-priority challenges around the world?*

Background: USAID recognized the need to expand the reach and impact of a relatively small agency in addressing high-priority global issues and to leverage the vast number of potential partners and collaborators in contributing to solving problems.

Innovation Solution:
- USAID launched, in conjunction with the Bill and Melinda Gates Foundation, the Global Innovation Exchange (GIE) with support from government, nongovernmental organizations, industry, academia, and international partners including Australia and South Korea to collaborate on solutions to major global issues.
- GIA is an online marketplace for innovators, experts, and funders to share valuable resources to accelerate global development innovation and global development and issues beyond those that USAID can address alone.
- GIE provided resources, links to articles, case studies, events, programs, organizations, and posts to share information furthering high-priority topics of global interest.

Lessons Learned:
- GIE grew into the largest database of global development innovations, with 16,000+ innovations and thousands of contributors.
- GIE grew to feature a funding directory, highlighting more than $3.5 billion in funding opportunities for innovations through a curated, filterable database.
- GIE ran a pitch contest to support innovators in honing their investment pitches to potential funders.
- In May 2020 GIE launched a COVID-19 Innovation Hub in response to the pandemic to source and supply related innovations.
- Due to lack of funding, the program was closed in the fall of 2021.

- **Saboteurs:** The person(s) threatened by the innovation project or program or its need for resources. Determining the pain points of a saboteur's job can help you understand why they are acting as a saboteur. Talking to the saboteur to find common ground and goals and can be an effective way to turn a foe into an ally and neutralize their negative behavior Talking to the saboteur can be fruitful, providing insights into your project or program. Using clear, transparent, and measurable communication with the saboteur creates an environment where obfuscation, evasion, and stalling tactics aren't successful. Alerting others, especially leadership, about the saboteur's behavior can unite forces against such actions and allow your innovation efforts to proceed. Plus, leadership may be able to reverse any stalling or undermining tactics the saboteur has used.

FIGURE 5.1 STAKEHOLDER MAP

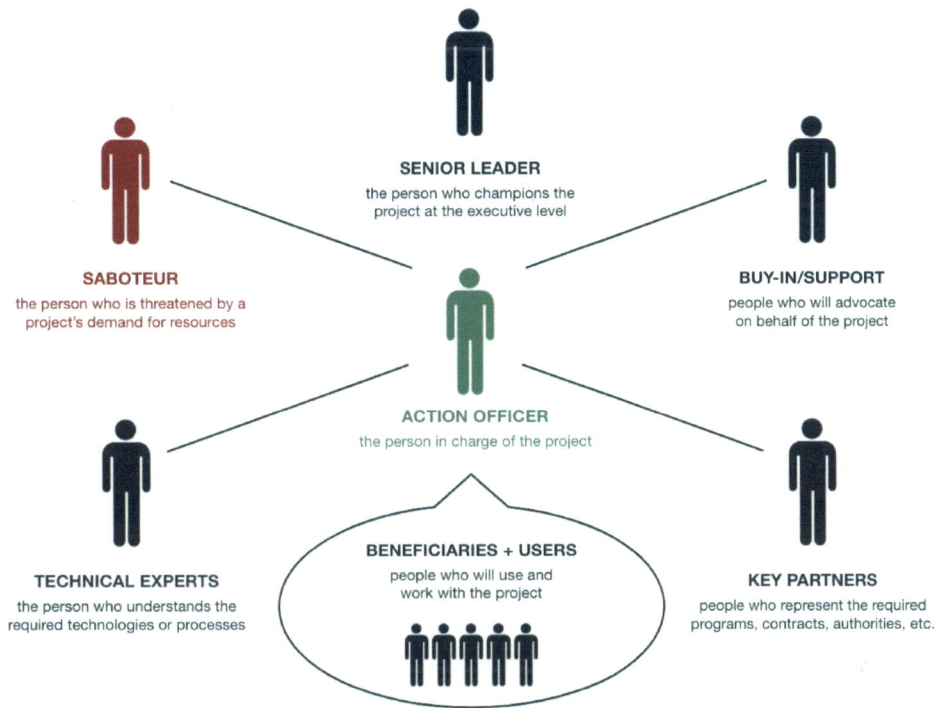

SENIOR LEADER
the person who champions the
project at the executive level

SABOTEUR
the person who is threatened by a
project's demand for resources

BUY-IN/SUPPORT
people who will advocate
on behalf of the project

ACTION OFFICER
the person in charge of the project

BENEFICIARIES + USERS
people who will use and
work with the project

TECHNICAL EXPERTS
the person who understands the
required technologies or processes

KEY PARTNERS
people who represent the required
programs, contracts, authorities, etc.

5.4 Mapping Stakeholders

A stakeholder map describes the key relationships involved in your innovation effort and clearly illustrates those who are most important for—or most threatened by—your innovation efforts. Consciously mapping your stakeholders lets you establish who inhabits each role, who is an obvious ally and advocate, and who needs to be cultivated more closely. The stakeholder map provides a guide to your most important relationships and to those with whom you should communicate more frequently and effectively. Building strong relationships with your stakeholders should be a fundamental concern; being methodical in identifying and understanding potential saboteurs can prevent serious missteps and allow you to rebuild critical relationships.

Creating a map of your stakeholders will provide an illuminating look at the innovation landscape within and outside of your organization. Inevitably, you will discover allies, advocates, and potential partnerships you had not been aware of. Whenever you are integrating new team members, starting a new project, discovering a new problem, or incubating a solution, turn to your stakeholder map to identify the relevant stakeholders, their expectations, and relationships. It can assist you by highlighting whom you need to influence to ensure the success of your Innovation Pipeline as well as areas of risk for your program and projects.

5.5 The Importance of Stakeholders

Stakeholders have the ability to make your innovation effort a success or a failure; they should always be considered in making any decisions or before starting any new project. If your stakeholders don't feel fully informed or are confused about your actions or motivations, they may actively try to kill your efforts before you've even begun your new project.

5.6 Creating a Stakeholder Map

Your map can include not only your stakeholders, but also their missions, interests, pain points, challenges, and potential pitfalls to better describe them. This more detailed stakeholder map will allow you and your team to communicate with your stakeholders more effectively. By clearly defining the issues of greatest importance to them, you can your tailor your messages to address their needs.

Creating stakeholder maps can be an individual or a group exercise, but it is often helpful to have your innovation team map stakeholders together, so each team member can learn from the group discussions and can bring to the team new or illuminating information that could sway the collective opinion about where a stakeholder should live on the map.

5.7 Communicating with Stakeholders

Communicating effectively with stakeholders so they understand your vision, goals, plans, programs, projects, successes, and failures, and are as committed to them as you are, is key to innovation success.

Determine how and what to communicate to each stakeholder in creating a common understanding. Understand and plan what method of communication will be most effective for each stakeholder, whether in-person discussions or drop-ins, email, interagency blog posts and updates, scheduled or unscheduled meetings, written or in-person task force summaries, weekly agency bulletins, or any other means you have found to be successful at your own agency. The frequency with which you communicate is important, but regularity and consistency are fundamental. Effective communications are almost never considered too frequent or too repetitious; overcommunicating is rarely detrimental.

Also plan for how you will take in the feedback offered by stakeholders, whether you plan to act on the input or not. At the very least, responding and acknowledging the feedback will win the respect of your stakeholder and will open the door for more exchanges and hopefully future collaboration. If the input is worthy of incorporating into your pipeline processes, activities, or projects, share the source of inspiration with your team, which will help in creating the collaborative environment you seek. In this way you can create innovators all around you as you march along your innovation path.

Module 5 Key Takeaways

- Senior support for your innovation effort is critical.

- Stakeholders can make your innovation effort a success or a failure and should always be considered when making decisions.

- Mapping stakeholders reveals potential allies, advocates, and saboteurs.

- Your stakeholder map can include not only your stakeholders but also their missions, interests, pain points, challenges, and potential pitfalls.

- The map provides a guide to your most important relationships and those with whom you should communicate more frequently and effectively.

EXERCISE: MAPPING YOUR STAKEHOLDERS

This exercise will help you identify and understand the many stakeholders in your innovation organization.

Who is your senior leader? _____

Who is your sponsor? _____

Who is the project/program owner? _____

Who are the beneficiaries and users of the project/program?

1 _____
2 _____
3 _____

From whom do you need buy-in and support?

1 _____
2 _____
3 _____
4 _____
5 _____

Who are your technical experts (IT, acquisition, legal, policy, HR, etc.)?

1 _____
2 _____
3 _____
4 _____
5 _____

Who can be key partners?

1 _____
2 _____
3 _____
4 _____
5 _____
6 _____

Who might be saboteurs?

1 _____
2 _____
3 _____

What communication methods should you use and to whom should you communicate with regularly?

_____

_____

_____

EXERCISE: BUILDING YOUR STAKEHOLDER COMMUNICATION PLAN

This exercise will help you craft a way to communicate with each of your stakeholders groups. Ideally, you will work closely with your agency's communications or public affairs experts to create a powerful plan.

Specifically, who are the stakeholders you need to communicate with?

_____
_____
_____
_____
_____
_____
_____
_____
_____

What are the mechanisms you will use to communicate?

_____
_____
_____
_____

What is the frequency with which you will communicate?

_____
_____

What is the feedback loop for these communications?

_____
_____
_____
_____

How will you incorporate this feedback into your plans?

_____
_____
_____
_____

How will you communicate the results of the feedback to your stakeholders?

_____
_____
_____
_____

TOOLS TO SUPPORT AN INNOVATION PIPELINE

6.1 Introduction

Thus far in this book, you have learned a lot, and you have accomplished a lot. Your goal is to build the "best, least worst solution that works," whether you are trying to bring about innovation within your existing organization, have been asked to be part of an innovation team, or are standing up your own innovation effort to solve mission problems. In building your innovation effort to include an Innovation Pipeline that helps your agency achieve mission impact, you have made a great deal of progress.

In Modules 1 and 2 you've considered the various elements of the Innovation Pipeline, including crafting an innovation strategy, and have begun thinking about the inputs, activities, and outputs within each of the five steps of the pipeline. You've learned in Module 3 about innovation models you can emulate and in Module 4 about the components to include in your pipeline, including the necessary people, partnerships, acquisition authorities, funding, and various forms of agency support you may need. And in Module 5 you've considered and mapped the important stakeholders of your pipeline and identified which relationships need to be cultivated, maintained, and attended to.

In this module, we'll consider innovation tools and methodologies to support the steps in building your innovation pipeline as well as how to better leverage commercial resources in this endeavor. There are many steps needed to craft your innovation approach, but remember you can scale all elements to match both your existing and future capacities and resources.

6.2 Leveraging Tools to Drive Innovation

Not all the tools mentioned in this module will be appropriate for your specific pipeline or needed to build your solutions. Use these resources and ways of approaching innovation as you see fit, and don't be afraid to tailor them to meet the various steps of your pipeline and the mission needs of your organization. Perhaps some of the specific tools highlighted here or in the Resources listed at the end of this book will guide you and your team to more effectively approach the challenges you face in instrumenting your pipeline.

Innovation Methodologies

These methodologies are ways of thinking about innovation and enabling us to approach our work in a manner that prioritizes the behaviors of innovation: a focus on end users, working with speed, taking risks, and quickly pivoting when we see our current path isn't moving us toward successful and mission-driven solutions. Innovation methodologies rise and fall from favor over time, but those that achieve results will always stand the test of time. All of the methodologies and techniques highlighted here have roots in the commercial sector; many of them emanated from Japanese manufacturing in the 1950s and then were discovered in the 1970s and 1980s by industry experts who sought to increase profits, often through improved productivity. The commercial sector will almost always be the originator of new ways of thinking and operating, due to its constant drive to create and increase revenue. Design companies in particular are great sources of new ways to approach thinking about customers. Government can learn much by studying how the commercial sector works and thinks.

Innovation approaches from the commercial sector can usually be easily translated to government innovation thinking. For instance, rather than focusing on the customer, as in the commercial sector, in government we focus on the end users, who may be critical infrastructure sector workers, law enforcement officials, human services providers, or intelligence officers and warfighters. Instead of focusing on customer value and purchasing of commercial products, think instead of mission focus and mission impact. And instead of envisioning developing widgets that will be sold to a customer, think of developing a tool or a policy or a process that will be used by the end user.

The following methodologies tend to support one of two parts of the Innovation Pipeline—either better understanding the innovation problem or better creating an appropriate solution. For further information on these methodologies, please see the Resources at the end of this book.

UNDERSTANDING END USERS AND THEIR NEEDS

Design thinking is a way of thinking and associated actions that create deep knowledge and understanding of the end user's problem, such that a superior solution can be crafted to solve the end user's challenges. Design thinking focuses on the user's experience, understanding at each step of the process their pain points and where they experience challenges. By listening carefully and empathizing with the user's experience, you can consider and reevaluate what the user's problem truly is and how to approach creating a solution. And by talking with a wide range of end users, you can learn about a wide range of challenges in order to create a better solution to those challenges.

For example, you could use a design thinking approach to improve the user experience for blood donation. How might you make it easier for the donor to sign up to give blood, get an appointment, and find a donation location; speed the check-in and identity verification process; and make the blood donation itself less painful and faster? To re-engineer this process, you could select several blood donors to interview, listening to and carefully recording their experiences in giving blood and what the process entailed. You could videotape donors during the process as another means of collecting information. You might interview enough donors that you could craft specific "archetypes" representing collections of end users (for example, "busy tech-savvy professional" or "donor who doesn't speak English") so that you can solve the specific problems of each (for example, making sign-up easier via an app or ensuring instructions are given in other languages).

The Hasso Plattner Institute of Design (known as the Stanford d.school), a foundational source of innovation approaches, conceptualized a design thinking process we can emulate (although this process recently has been modified); the five steps are empathizing with the end user, defining their pain points, ideating and prototyping potential solutions, and testing the solutions with end users.

Design thinking includes experimentation on and testing of the prototype solutions, then soliciting feedback from your original end users to see if the solutions you created are better suited to address the pain points you unearthed in discovery. The discovery/prototype/test process is iterative; as you develop potential solutions, you return to end user conversations to further refine your ideas and resulting solutions. The book The Designing for Growth Field Book (Liedtka and Ogilvie, 2011, Columbia Business School Publishing), provides a plethora of techniques and tips to maximize your design thinking activities.

USE CASE 8: U.S. Navy's Tactical Advancements for the Next Generation (TANG)
Innovation Problem to be Solved: *How might the DoD use human-centered design approaches to tackle difficult DOD mission challenges?*

Background: In 2014, Program Executive Office Integrated Warfare System 5.0 (PEO IWS 5.0) established a new approach to innovation using design thinking to deliver mission solutions.

Innovation Solution:
- TANG uses a warfighter-centered collaborative process that brings together a diverse group of stakeholders, including civilians, contractors, enlisted and officer personnel with commercial partners to tackle challenges through innovation and experts solving complex challenges.
- With a sponsor, multidisciplinary project teams conduct immersive research to frame a problem and better understand pain points.
- TANG runs "Design Events" that brings a myriad of stakeholders together to develop prototypes to address the mission problems.
- Research, end user input, emerging technology, and case studies are used to frame structured brainstorming and rapid prototyping efforts.
- Example of TANG transitioned prototypes include a military-grade submarine periscope joystick with commercial controller developed at a fraction of the cost of standard military equipment.

Lessons Learned:
- Mitigating early risks and accelerating solutions to the field, using a design thinking approach, results in rapid solutions delivered at a lower cost.
- Real-time collaboration between end users, designers, developers, acquisition professionals and senior leaders significantly hastens more traditional and slow acquisition processes.
- Minimally viable products speed acquisition and can be used in nontechnical areas such as policy and training.

Lean methodology has its origins in the Toyota Production System in the 1950s, which emphasized streamlining manufacturing by eliminating waste and creating value to the customer. Lean underscores understanding what the customer is willing to pay for, understanding and evaluating the process, and eliminating irrelevant tasks that don't add value for the customer. Lean Six Sigma has similar roots, with a focus on reducing flaws in the manufacturing process.

Building on Lean methodology is Lean Startup methodology, an approach to increase the success of startup companies. Lean Startup was developed from Steve Blank's customer discovery concept articulated in his *The Four Steps to the Epiphany* and refined for the startup market by Blank's student Eric Ries in *The Lean Startup*. Central to the methodology is continuous learning, developing and refining your solution based on customer needs, or "getting out of the building." By advocating for need assessment and developing and testing products according to customer needs, through the minimally viable product (MVP), the method builds companies that deliver customer value. Lean Startup has proven a successful method in creating sustainable businesses.

Although created by and for the commercial market, both Lean and Lean Startup espouse ideas significantly relevant to federal innovation. The relentless focus on understanding, creating, and delivering value to the customer is directly applicable to federal workers. The motivation to deliver mission results to end users ("customers") is analogous, whether the federal end users are critical infrastructure sector workers, law enforcement officials, human services providers, or intelligence officers and warfighters.

SOLUTION DEVELOPMENT APPROACHES

Design sprint is a strict five-day process for creating a solution, in which some elements of design thinking and agile are used. Former Google designer Jake Knapp created the design sprint to ensure that speed, that essential ingredient in innovation, drove the development process. Design sprints gather key stakeholders to collaboratively develop solutions using the following schedule:

- Day 1: Understand the problem and end user
- Day 2: Sketch possible solutions
- Day 3: Evaluation the solutions and decide which to pursue
- Day 4: Create a minimally viable product
- Day 5: Test the MVP with end users

Although user experience is important in the design sprint, the emphasis is on quickly finding and creating solutions and using a key group of stakeholders to develop them, at the expense of further exploring user needs.

The concepts of agile and rapid, both referring to the development and delivery of solutions (usually technology), are often are used interchangeably. Both describe approaches to creating and scaling products. Agile emphasizes iterative, incremental, and speedy changes using existing mechanisms to adapt quickly; "sprints," or quick and focused bursts of work, are central to the iterative process used in agile, cumulatively adding up to significant product changes, with partial product delivery made regularly, to better met customer needs. Decision-making is collaborative and pushed to the lowest levels possible to prevent roadblocks and impediments to decisions. Rapid, in contrast, puts less emphasis on understanding requirements and more on the creation of prototypes, which may mean using precious resources that may not result in an appropriately developed tool. If you are developing a technology, agile may be a more useful approach, as all government resources are costly, increasing the need to get the best mission-oriented solution as quickly as possible.

In the federal innovation world, agile and rapid are often used to describe acquisition and procurement authorities and processes. The concept of speeding manufacturing and product delivery in the commercial world become popular in federal acquisition and in Congress and translated easily into improvements that could make the lumbering federal acquisition process easier.

Scrum is a framework to facilitate agile development by planning and executing projects. Scrum uses frequent communication between product owners and the development team to prevent roadblocks in the development process, like government "stand-up" meetings—usually short daily meetings to coordinate and deconflict efforts to ensure common situational awareness. Similarly, there is a component, essentially a government "hotwash," of reviewing successes and failures in the project. Communications track pending, in progress, and completed production work.

Kanban, which uses boards to represent development and production work items, is a visual technique for tracking all the elements of work to be completed and that have been completed, rather than discarding elements once completed. Having this history of development allows for better insight into critical decisions once the project is completed. NavalX's Centers for Adaptive Warfighting teach the concepts of scrum, agile, and human-centered design.

If you are indeed working on the development of a technology and have a team of developers to assist with this process, thoroughly explore these methodologies and techniques to find those that will be of greatest use in achieving results for your mission, given your agency's strengths and resources.

Government innovation, although nascent, is leveraging the resources from its close cousin, industry innovation, which, par for the course, has taken the lead. A plethora of tools exist to help you create your innovation approach. Remember that the goal is to find the right tool for the right problem and to apply it at the right time. In choosing the right tools to crafting your innovation approach, start by determining what decisions you need to make to understand the information you need to gather. Doing so drives the activities you'll need to undertake, which helps you decide which tools to use.

Foundational to government innovation are Steve Blank's books *The Four Steps to the Epiphany* and *The Startup Owner's Manual*, and his innovation blog (https://steveblank.com/). Although originally part of commercial sector and creator of eight successful startup companies, the Stanford University entrepreneurship professor directed his passion for service to the nation by translating his concepts for commercial innovation to government innovation. His "Red Queen Problem" blog post is a seminal government innovation touchstone. Eric Ries's *The Learn Startup* is another important resource.

Alex Osterwalder's Strategyzer series (*Business Model Generation*, *Value Proposition Design*, *The Invincible Company*, among many others, with accompanying classes), although intended for the commercial sector and for startups in particular, holds great value for the federal innovation market. Osterwalder developed the concept of the Mission Model Canvas (MMC; see Appendix J) as well as the Value Proposition Canvas (VPC; see Appendix K). The MMC is based on the Business Model Canvas, a fundamental tool in creating startups, which focuses on customer needs and creating a product that will meet those needs. Similarly, the MMC template captures the end user's mission and needs and helps craft a solution that will provide a powerful solution. The VPC helps craft a solution that examines end user pain points, their "jobs to be done," and how potential solutions could solve these pain points.

Another significant contributors to commercial sector innovation, and therefore to government innovation, is IDEO, one of the earliest and most successful design companies and the creator of many hundreds of important design innovations. This Silicon Valley-based company popularized the design thinking approach and made the customer experience central to design creation. IDEO made its design thinking approach transparent to other commercial companies and ultimately the public, offering collaborative platforms, educational programs, and multiple books on design thinking, in the process changing the way in which many of us think.

When considering the resources and tools described above and in the book's appendices, don't lose sight of several key points:

- These tools should make concepts clearer and easier to replicate in your own Innovation Pipeline.
- Understand both how to use the tools and how to tailor them to your specific Innovation Pipeline.
- As your innovation problems change, so too should the tools you use.
- As your innovation solutions change, so too should the tools you use.

A key tenet of innovation is the openness to constant learning and refining your understanding of and approaches to solving end user problems. These tools can give you new ways to think about your end users, your problems, and your potential solutions in realizing mission impact.

FIGURE 6.2 IMPORTANT BOOKS ON INNOVATION

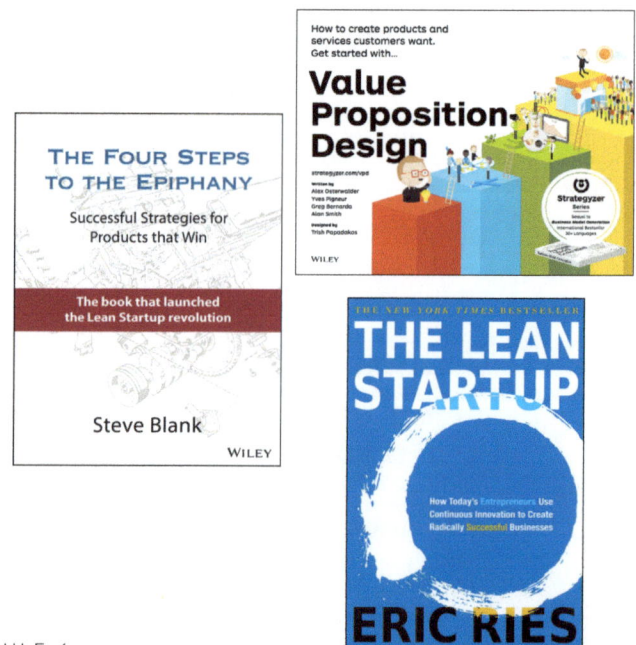

6.3 Why It's Important to Get Commercial Technology into Government

In thinking about finding solutions to your agency's problems, and in thinking of the resources available to solve these problems, it is helpful to understand that the U.S. government is no longer the primary funder and developer of technology and systems. Industry expenditures on technology research and development surpassed those of the federal government in approximately 1980, and industry currently more than triples government spending. If we add venture capital funding of dual-use technologies, which are applicable in both commercial and government markets, the figures become staggering. Many of the best experimental and emerging technologies are being created by small and young companies. Simply put, to access the best tools, you must be open to including commercial technology.

FIGURE 6.3 U.S. GOVERNMENT VS INDUSTRY RESEARCH AND DEVELOPMENT FUNDING, IN BILLIONS

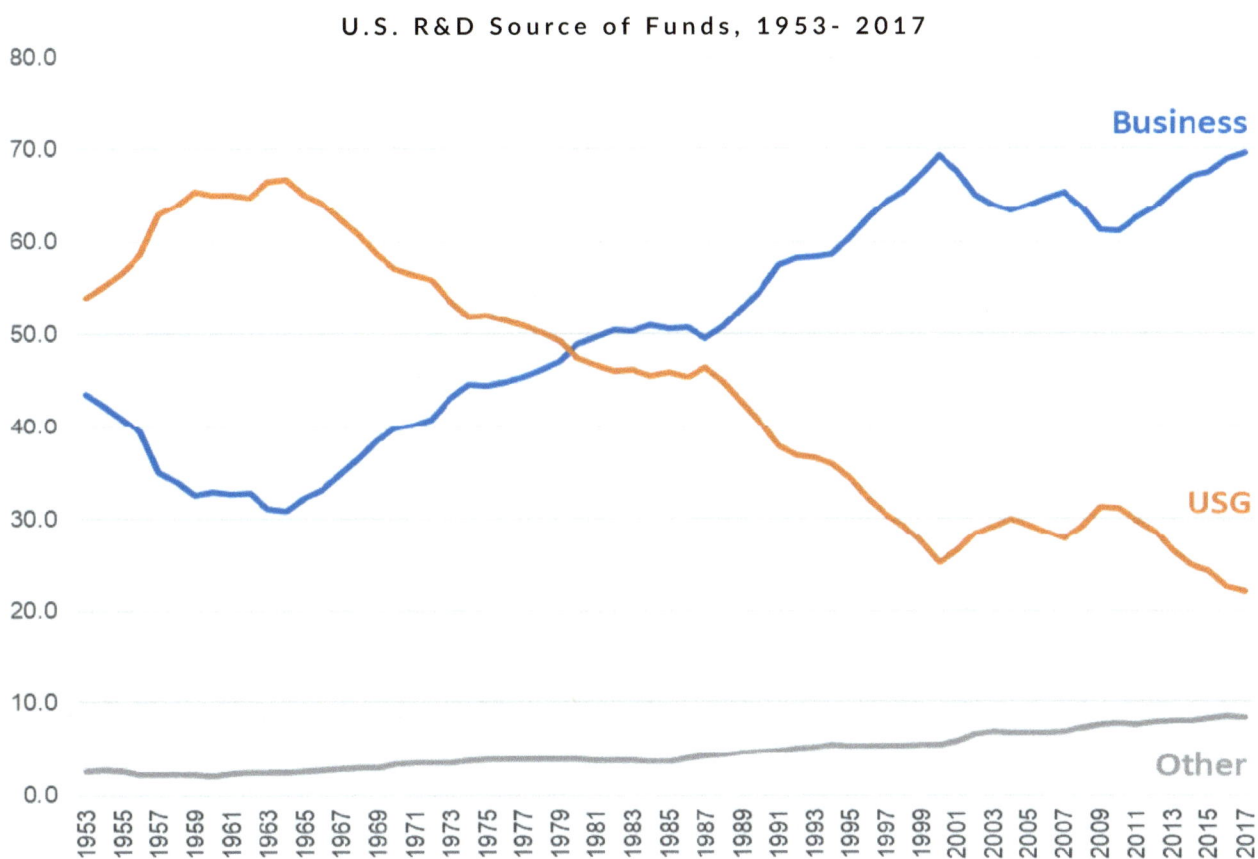

U.S. R&D Source of Funds, 1953- 2017

CONSIDERATIONS FOR CHOOSING INDUSTRY PARTNERS

So how can you efficiently and effectively acquire commercial technologies and capabilities for government use? First, understand how to judge the companies you are contemplating working with, whether they be startups, small businesses, or prime contractors, who may be working with subcontractors focused on more experimental technologies. There are advantages and disadvantages to working with each type of company, and government incentives for working with each type vary. For instance, the size of an organization is important; risk increases when working with small companies and decreases with larger companies. You need to be able to appropriately calculate what the government can gain—or lose—in working with the company in order to reduce the level of risk.

It's also important to understand the viewpoints of different companies. In larger companies, profit is less of a motivation than minimizing the potential for loss. Weighted government purchasing guidelines cap company gross earnings to less than 50% of commercial standards. And many government buying strategies penalize good cost performance in exchange for low risk of delivery.

When working with government, industry is looking for various things: a commitment to work collaboratively together to achieve a mutually agreed upon and contracted capability, service, or tool; a stable, low-friction, low-pain relationship with government and its employees; and the opportunity for funding as well as the opportunity to grow the relationship toward future partnerships.

STARTUPS

If considering working with startups, you should determine the level of risk in working with the startup, particularly in getting delivery of the contracted capability. Before contracting with a company, ask the following questions:

- Does the company and its product(s) have traction in the government space?
- Do they have credibility?
- Can you validate their ability to perform by seeking references from people you know and trust?
- What is their annual reoccurring revenue (ARR)?

In general, startup do not have the stability government usually seeks in a partnership as the risk in delivering a capability is too great. Yet you may only find the type of capability you seek with such a higher-risk company.

When working with government, startups face considerable risk. Federal acquisition cycles are often too long and too complex to be worth the investment of time and energy. Government funding is often transitory and can't be counted on as a regular source of income. The acquisition process has many incremental barriers that must be overcome, which makes the process onerous, and each federal agency has different rules that must be followed. Government is not transparent—and usually can't be transparent, given traditional federal acquisition regulations. Simply put, the FAR was neither created nor modified over the decades with innovation in mind.

SMALL BUSINESSES

When considering small businesses, determine if the company is stable enough to deliver your contracted capability in your expected time frame and whether it has the ability and capacity to meet your requirements:

- What is their annual reoccurring revenue (ARR)?
- Do they have the capacity to deliver your requirements, or can they procure the skills and tools to deliver your requirements?

Understand that if the company doesn't currently have the capability, it will take them time to find and develop those resources, which may or may not be of the quality you seek.

PRIMES

In working with primes, there is much less risk in terms of their stability and ability to deliver the required contracted capability. Focus on the overall health of the company, and whether it has made the appropriate investments in its own capabilities, balancing that with return on the investment. What is their return on invested capital (ROIC)?

It may be easier to work with prime contractors that already have contracted emerging or commercial technology, which are subprimes to them. Primes have existing contract vehicles and dedicated specialists who know how to work on them efficiently and effectively; they have established systems, infrastructure, and processes; and they have business development teams that can be dedicated to your agency as their area of responsibility. They may have knowledge of previous work done with your agency and their past performance, including the good, the bad, and the truly ugly. They have strategists who assist them in protecting their intellectual property and in working collaboratively with the federal government, both in creating contracts and in awarding contracts to their subcontractors. And their agreement with their subcontractors will have a strategic approach for appropriating the intellectual property and managing their cashflow appropriately.

In working with a company, regardless of its size or maturity, there are important factors to remember. Involve your senior leaders and prime leadership in discussions, and include legal counsel. Engage your legal and procurement stakeholders from the beginning. Programs should be a partnership, with program objectives and key results revised as the program or project matures. Verify potential partner capabilities before you commit to ensure situational awareness and the understanding of your project's constraints. Ensure the company's technology is relatively mature to diminish the risk of costly and time-sucking modifications. Select the right people for both the government and the company teams who have the qualifications and ability to lead your project to success.

Help your partners succeed in meeting your mutual goals by establishing clear goals and objectives, specifying the "what" and not the "how." Once your project is under way, give the company the leeway to do what it is that they do best. You've hired them for a reason, so give them the latitude to deliver. Communicate that sometimes failure is acceptable, if it means learning more about the project in the process and progress is continued towards delivery. Help them recover quickly from any failures so you can continue to progress. Create win/win situations by building in incentives for the company that help you meet your mutual goals. Plan reserves within the program to mitigate the inevitable challenges that arise in the process. And, most importantly, don't let an entrenched culture within your agency kill the potential for using commercial products and technology to achieve mission results.

Module 6 Key Takeaways

- Not all the tools mentioned in this module will be appropriate in crafting your specific pipeline or will be needed in building your solutions.

- Government can learn much by studying how the commercial sector works and thinks.

- Design thinking is a way of thinking and associated actions that create deep knowledge and understanding of the end user's problem, such that a superior solution can be crafted to solve the end user's challenges.

- In choosing the right tools to crafting your innovation approach, start by determining what decision you need to make to understand the information you need to gather.

- It may be easier to work with prime contractors, which already have contracted emerging or commercial technology.

CREATING AND MAINTAINING AN INNOVATION CULTURE

7.1 Introduction

Recall that the essence of innovation is creating a culture that accepts and encourages change, where everyone recognizes when change needs to take place and is ready and willing to make the necessary change. Thus, in creating an innovative culture, it is vital that you, your team, your senior leaders, and your stakeholders are vigilant in looking for opportunities to make the right changes at the right time to bring about innovation.

Changing an organization's culture requires brave individuals who are willing to put their reputation on the line.

To break an existing culture and replace it with a more innovative culture, focus on those who are most integral in effecting change, usually middle management or program managers, or what is known as "the frozen middle." This group is motivated to achieve the existing goals of their team, which may conflict with innovation activities, so there is a tendency for some middle management to be less likely to accept new ways of doing things or to disturb existing processes or resources. By focusing on enlisting support for culture change from middle management, you can more easily affect processes and resource allocation to align with your vision of innovation or innovative solutions.

7.2 Getting Innovation Adopted

Nothing in a career is more discouraging and disheartening than doing a lot of work, only to have it ignored or underutilized. By determining how you can extend your efforts beyond yourself and your team, you can significantly increase your chances of bringing about true change throughout your organization.

- Ensure you have strong leadership support for innovation, including directly communicating to the entire organization that innovation is a priority. Leadership support to help push through the inevitable roadblocks and to achieve buy-in from important stakeholders is vital to ensuring the success of your program.
- Find like-minded "influencers" and key stakeholders who can be advisors to your program and who will serve as messengers throughout your organization. Keep them as strong advocates who know your program well and who will speak to the importance of innovation and your program in many venues.
- Explain to your team, stakeholders, partners, and end users what needs to happen throughout the innovation process to keep making progress on your problems, program and projects. Often, your colleagues will not be able to envision an innovation process, so providing them an overall vision, the steps to be taken along with the specifics within each step, and expected outcomes will go far in helping them actively participate in creating your vision.
- Provide your team, stakeholders, partners, and end users practical tools with examples that will assist them in executing the steps of the Innovation Pipeline, so they have a strong model to follow in creating problem, project, and program success.
- Focus on the mission, the common long-term goals and objectives, and how your innovation projects can help achieve these goals.
- Communicate frequently to every level of your organization—including leadership, stakeholders, executors of the work, beneficiaries, and end users—so they understand your vision, the progress

being made, the roadblocks that are being experienced, and the successes that are achieved. Communication is fundamental to creating buy-in and in ameliorating the challenges you might face in bringing innovation to your organization.

- Look out for potential roadblocks and saboteurs, and try to proactively address such obstacles before they disrupt or damage your short- or long-term goals.

7.3 Instrumenting Your Innovation Pipeline

By properly instrumenting your Innovation Pipeline, you can ensure you have a robust and promisingly full, yet not overwhelming, pipeline to maximize your potential in succeeding with both individual problems and an overall innovation program. Models within the startup and venture capital worlds show us that for every ten projects, properly resourced, it is reasonable to expect that only one will be successful for any number of reasons. Recognize and accept that this level of failure is simply unheard of within government; because taxpayer dollars support federal efforts, each project or program is expected to succeed. Prepare yourself and your leadership, team, stakeholders, and end users for what may feel like an unacceptably high rate of "failure." However, it is only by starting out with a large number of problems that you can arrive at the best mission solutions.

By creating sound decision criteria at each step of the Innovation Pipeline, you can manage the rate of problems moving through the pipeline so that it aligns with the resources you have allocated to the problems or solutions. The decision criteria at each stage should allow an appropriate number of problems to progress to the next stage. If you have too few problems entering each stage, you will not end up with an adequate number of high-quality solutions to consider; too many problems at each stage means you may not have adequate bandwidth or resources to manage the flood of problems and solutions you are confronted with.

FIGURE 7.1 WINNOWING THE INNOVATION PIPELINE

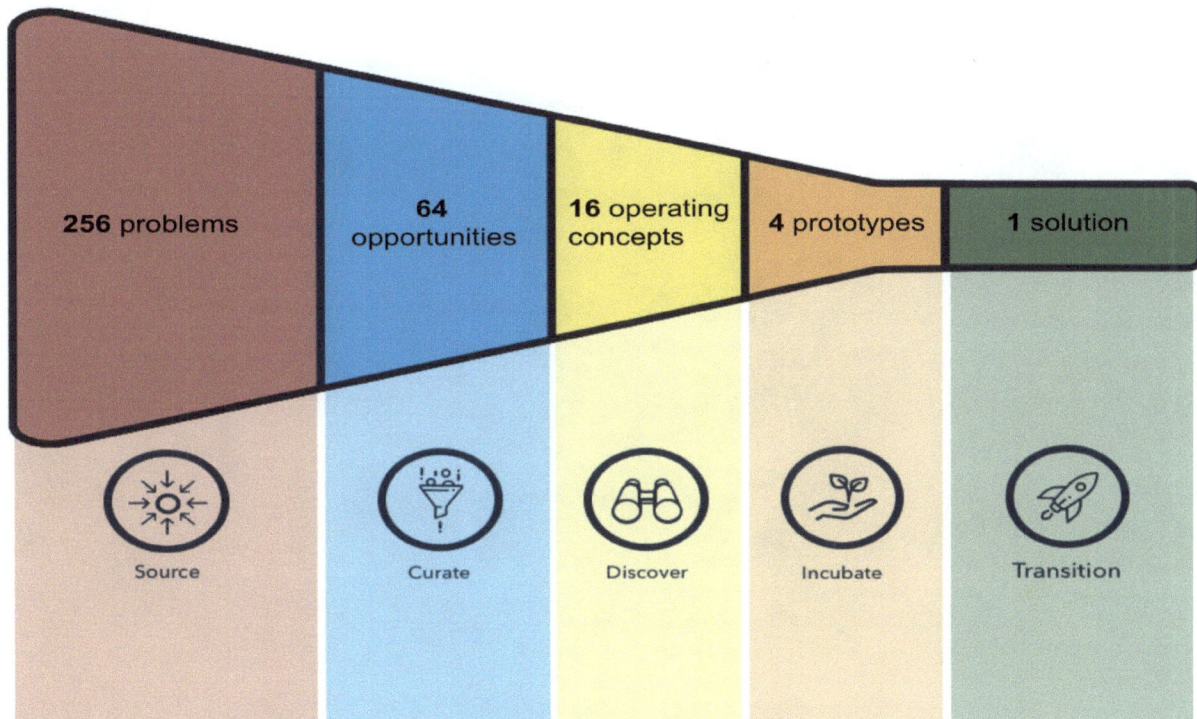

256 problems | 64 opportunities | 16 operating concepts | 4 prototypes | 1 solution

Source | Curate | Discover | Incubate | Transition

7.4 Monitoring Progress of Your Innovation Pipeline

Regular monitoring of your Innovation Pipeline is required to confirm you have an appropriate flow of problems and solutions. If you have too few resources (whether personnel, detailees, contractors, or funding) to adequately manage the number of problems and potential solutions, close the aperture of your Innovation Pipeline by carefully considering the decision criteria you are using for each step of the pipeline and making the criteria for entering each step more rigorous to ensure you are allowing fewer projects to enter. Conversely, if you have too few problems and solutions coming through your pipeline, open the aperture by reviewing the decision criteria and making them less stringent to allow more problems and solutions to flow through.

Using appropriate metrics to monitor each step of the Innovation Pipeline is important; see Module 8 for further information. Additionally, you can determine whether technology solutions are appropriately mature to move to the next stages of the pipeline by measuring their investment readiness level (IRL) and adoption readiness level (ARL) as checkpoints between each stage of the pipeline. IRLs and ARLs are also covered in Module 8.

FIGURE 7.2 RESULTS OF THE INNOVATION PIPELINE

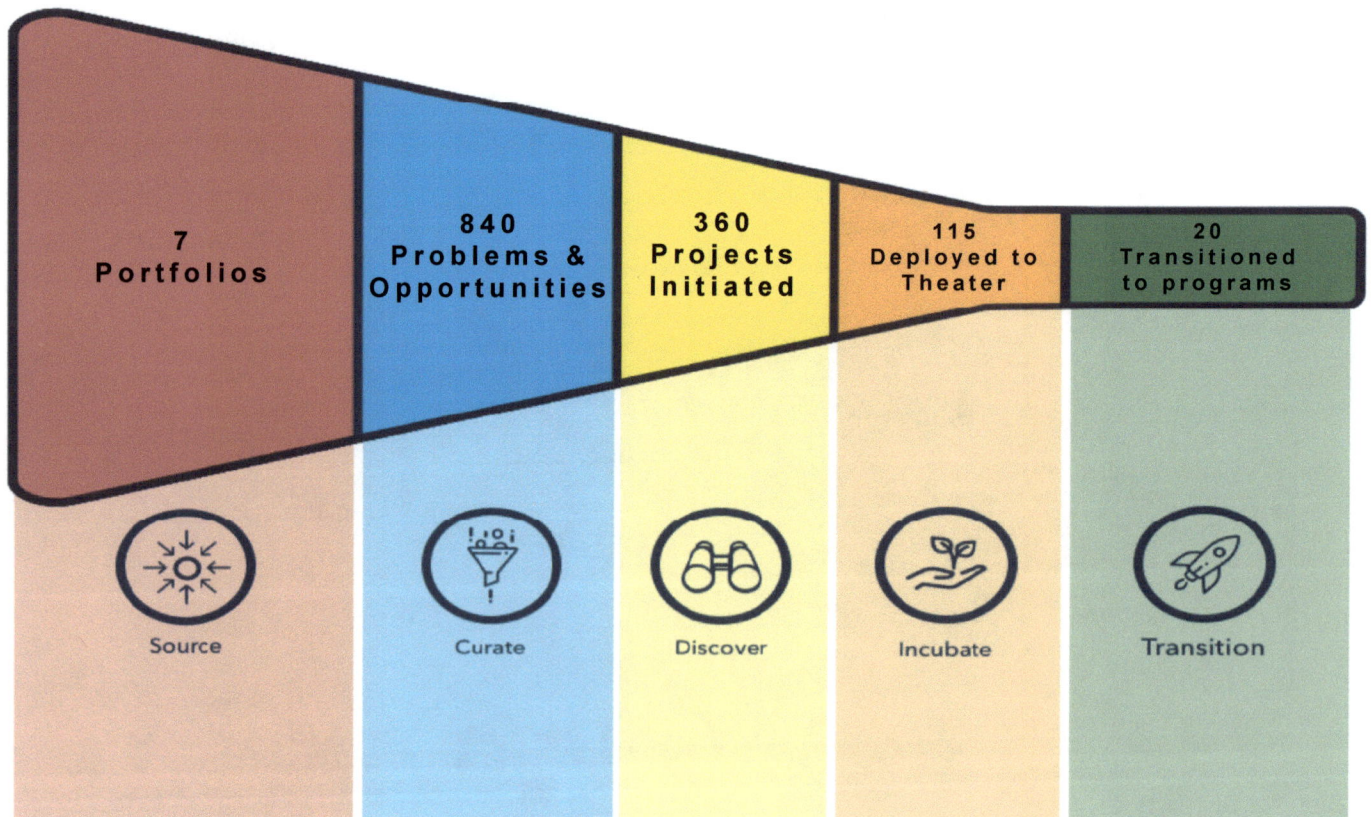

7 Portfolios	840 Problems & Opportunities	360 Projects Initiated	115 Deployed to Theater	20 Transitioned to programs
Source	Curate	Discover	Incubate	Transition

7.5 Using Your Stakeholders

Given your vast and growing network of contacts and stakeholders, it is helpful to gather them around specific problems and potential solutions to continue to grow and cultivate an appropriately large group, with many different perspectives. It is this collection of external perspectives that will expand your vision of how problems can be solved and how and where solutions can be developed, as well as give you connections to resources you had not imagined. Seek to cultivate advocates, not just allies, those who proactively drive your interests in ways that influence resourcing.

In addition, your cultivated stakeholder network can be a solid source of information regarding the progress of your innovation problems, proposed solutions, and your innovation program in general. Hearing multiple perspectives and data points about your program, and really listening to the feedback, will provide you insights you may not have received if you relied on just your own perspective and the opinions of your team and those in your inner circle. Rob Fitzpatrick's book, The Mom Test,4 provides useful advice on how to ensure you are hearing and capturing honest assessment of your efforts.

7.6 Project Management Under Fire

Your path toward innovation will not always be smooth. When you encounter obstacles, addressing the issues proactively is a much more effective technique than turning a blind eye and hoping projects will work out. Hope is not an effective plan! There are many effective ways to directly address challenges, including the following:

- Seek leadership guidance to ensure that your goals, vision, and plans are aligned with those of leadership. Be honest and complete in your assessment of the problems you are facing, and seek leadership support—or accept their assessment, as they no doubt have insights to which you may not have been privy.
- Use real data when assessing the project or the situation and sharing information to ensure you are describing the situation as accurately as possible.
- Seek honest feedback from leadership, stakeholders, project staff, and end users regarding the state of the project or program, asking questions to better understand their perspectives on the challenges you're facing.
- Talk to allies who support your vision and project efforts; the situation may not be as dire as it appears to you.

- If you are facing saboteurs, talk to them to understand their motivations for their lack of support or active undermining. You may be able to clear up a misunderstanding or discover an unstated common goal that can be met together.
- Propose alternative solutions to the current situation, or look to other projects for ideas and inspiration.
- Ask leadership, stakeholders, and end users for their ideas for possible solutions.
- Seek partnerships to help you avoid antagonism from possible competitors and to successfully manage what may be perceived as a rice bowl issue.
- Give away projects if this move will gain you advocates and save important resources. Losing a small battle, and gaining support in the process, may help you win the war.
- If evidence shows a project or program is not and cannot be made successful, quickly pivot away from it and move your resources toward other efforts.
- Recover gracefully. In your communications, highlight the positives while realistically recognizing the negatives. Focus on gaining advocates and supporters to be ready for the next challenge.

4Fitzpatrick, R. (2013). *The Mom Test: How to Talk to Customers and Learn If Your Business Is a Good Idea When Everyone Is Lying To You*. CreateSpace Independent Publishing Platform.

7.7 Killing a Project or Program

Sometimes a project, or even a program, may not work as efficiently or effectively as intended. In government, programs are seldom challenged and rarely killed, but may die a slow and painful death. Directly addressing the failure or lack of success of a project or program is powerful because it leads to action. Sometimes there is a fear of acknowledging that a project is not working. People become attached to their projects; many do not follow the rule of thumb to "never fall in love with your program." Accepting failure, however, is a critical part of the innovative mindset. You and your team must be willing to accept the possibility that a potential solution is not effective, or not able to solve a mission problem.

How can you effectively kill, or suggest killing, a project or even a program without demoralizing your team or sending a negative message about the importance of their collective effort? Hopefully from the start you have set expectations with leadership, project teams, stakeholders, and end users that not every solution or project will be, or should be, successful—if every innovation project you work on is successful, you may not be aiming high enough or trying to achieve game-changing results. Focus on the agency's mission, a rallying cry for the federal workforce, to highlight the gap between the vision and reality, and the fact that you are working together toward a common, overarching goal. And you can highlight the savings of both funding and resources that result from killing a project as a win for innovation, rather than a failure. Now those resources can be better used for a project with a better chance of success in creating mission impact.

Module 7 Key Takeaways

- Providing your innovation team an overall vision, the steps to be taken along with the specifics within each step, and expected outcomes will go far in helping them actively participate in creating your vision.

- Prepare yourself and your leadership, team, stakeholders, and end users for the inevitable "failures."

- Create sound decision criteria at each step of the Innovation Pipeline to manage the rate of problems moving through the pipeline so that it aligns with the resources you have allocated to the problems or solutions.

- Use real data when assessing the project or the situation and sharing information to ensure you are describing the situation as accurately as possible.

- Never fall in love with your program.

EXERCISE: MAPPING POTENTIAL ROADBLOCKS

This exercise will help you highlight potential roadblocks, which should be regularly assessed to determine whether they are hampering your innovation efforts and projects.

1. **Leadership Direction and Priorities:** Are your innovation program, projects, and solutions aligned with leadership strategy and priorities with agency mission?

2. **Changing User Needs:** Are your innovation program, projects, and solutions aligned to meet current end user needs and to fulfill their mission?

3. **Stakeholder Support:** Do your innovation program, projects, and solutions help your stakeholders achieve their strategy and priorities?

4. **Personnel:** Are your team members aligned with your innovation program, projects, and solutions?

5. **Funding:** Is there any change in the funding to support your innovation program, projects, and solutions? If so, why? What has changed in the agency, mission, or federal landscape to effect such a change?

6. **Existing Agency Programs and Projects:** Are your innovation program, projects, and solutions competing with other agency efforts? How can you align these efforts to find common goals?

7. **Partnerships:** Do your innovation program, projects, and solutions help your partners achieve their strategy and priorities?

8. **Legal:** Are your innovation program, projects, and solutions meeting legal challenges? If not, how can they be overcome?

9. **Security:** Are your innovation program, projects, and solutions meeting security challenges? If not, how can they be overcome?

METRICS THAT MATTER: OUTCOME-BASED PERFORMANCE

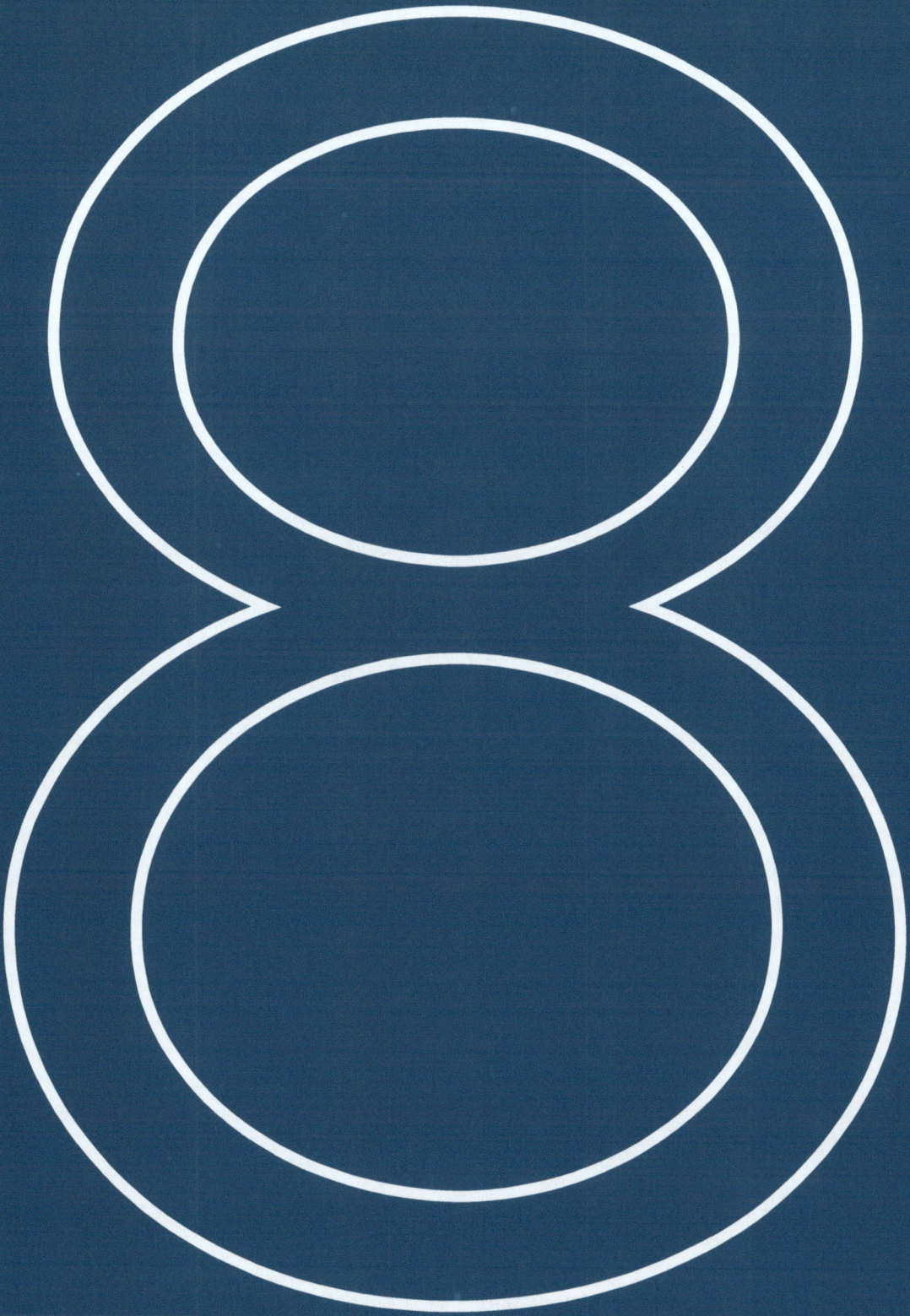

8.1 Introduction

Tracking the effectiveness and efficiency of your Innovation Pipeline with real and measurable data is essential to ensure success in meeting mission priorities and achieving mission impact. Metrics should be used to inform your senior leadership and sponsor about your program performance and progress and to alert them to your innovation and mission.

Tracking metrics can alert your action officers as to steps and activities within the pipeline that need increased attention and successful delivery and how to adjust the pipeline to maximize its efficiency and effectiveness in delivering mission impact.

8.2 What to Measure in Your Innovation Pipeline

In measuring your Innovation Pipeline, each of the pipeline elements (pipeline and infrastructure processes; activities, methodologies, and tools; data tracked; metrics; and operational support) requires its own metrics to adequately assess its performance. Suggested metrics for each stage are provide within this module. For further support, see Appendix L.

Speed is perhaps the most important metric to measure, both the amount of time it takes for each problem to pass through the pipeline and average time lines for problems and solutions to enter and exit each step within the pipeline. Assessing each step will help you determine when a step needs to be modified so it can be completed more quickly. Time is a finite resource; if it takes too long to transition solutions from the Innovation Pipeline

into programs of record to have real mission impact, it increases the risk of the solution not being adopted. Or, worse, your Innovation Pipeline could be perceived as not efficient in creating mission impact or as wasting agency resources in the attempt to do so.

Reviewing the steps of your entire Innovation Pipeline and the processes by which you realize the impact of the pipeline is different from reviewing the result, or the solutions it develops. The solutions developed by the pipeline, and their readiness to transition into the broader organization can be characterized by the measures of technology readiness level (TRL), investment readiness level (IRL), and adoption readiness level (ARL); these are covered in Section 8.6.

8.3 When to Measure Your Innovation Pipeline

Review the efficacy of your Innovation Pipeline on a regular basis, usually every 30 days, once your pipeline team, resources, and processes are established; it is not necessary to wait until the incubation stage to begin to measure your proposed solution.

A monthly analysis will give you sufficient data to track and analyze your progress so you can identify and perform any needed fine-tuning, updating, and adjustments on a timely basis. Only through reviewing the pipeline can you identify gaps in the process and execute remedies to shore

them up.

Measuring and reviewing the entire process will reveal how and where in the pipeline the most time and effort are being spent, so you can assess where adjustments need to be made to increase the efficiency and efficacy of your pipeline, and where your pipeline may be broken, in need of a wholesale correction. Only by removing yourself from the daily activities of the pipeline to complete a regular assessment is such a a holistic view possible.

8.4 Measuring the Impact of Your Innovation Pipeline

It is critical for mission success to measure the overall impact on mission your innovation efforts are having, rather than only measuring the activities and outputs of innovation of your Innovation Pipeline. To do so, return to the foundational documents that define your agency's mission and inform your agency's goals and priorities that you used to create the strategy for your pipeline.

These might include leadership and agency guidance and strategies, federal and congressional mandates, executive orders, and strategies. Aggregating all such documents will illustrate the agency's highest priorities and provide insights into how innovation can assist your agency in achieving mission. Your agency may have an office for performance metrics that can provide you insights into crafting impact metrics.

8.5 How to Measure the Steps of Your Innovation Pipeline

Recall the five steps of your Innovation Pipeline: sourcing, curation, discover, incubation, and transition. For each step, you should analyze the pipeline and infrastructure processes; activities, methodologies, and tools; data tracked; metrics; and operational support. Each step requires its own metrics to determine the relative functioning

and success. The following figure illustrates the types of metrics that can be useful to measure the effectiveness of each step in achieving the pipeline elements. Your specific pipeline metrics can be crafted to best highlight how you can achieve mission impact.

FIGURE 8.1 POSSIBLE METRICS FOR EACH STEP OF THE INNOVATION PIPELINE

Step	Metrics
Sourcing	• Number of active internal and external sourcing programs • Ratio of new sources netted from each event to those actually engaged in other parts of the pipeline over time (passive vs active connections) • Ratio of entities sourced to entities accepted into next phase (1:1 ration indicates a weak sourcing mechanism, 4:1 may is preferable)
Curation	• Ratio of problems / new concepts curated to those accepted into Discovery (1:1 reflects a weak pool; 4:1 is closer to historical norms from REF and H4D) • Ratio of problems / new concepts spread across Alex Osterwalder's portfolio map vs. 3 Horizons • Initial TRL / IRL and ARL established • Quality of teams in Discovery: how many meet minimum standards and remain intact?
Discovery	• Number of hypotheses and MVP's generated • Number of team pivots • Number and diversity of interviews conducted • TRL, IRL, and ARL at completion of Discovery • Number of external partners and internal parts of organization engaged
Incubation	• Ratio of teams in incubation to those gaining follow-on investment (for H1 teams maybe 2:1, H2 teams 4:1, H3 teams 10:1) • Change in TRL, IRL, and ARL of teams throughout Incubation and at departure to transition • Condensation: number of projects in discovery combined into one effort moving forward to incubation
Transition	• Ratio of teams receiving initial investment leaving incubation to those receiving follow-on investment (different ratios for H1, H2, and H3) • Ratio of teams in transition to those accepted in POR or theater sustainment (different ratios for H1, H2, and H3) • Average time spent in transition (shorter for H1, longer for H3)

8.6 How to Measure the Results of Your Innovation Pipeline

You will track different metrics depending on whether your solution is or is not a technology solution. Nontechnology solutions include policies, processes, authorities, tools such as playbooks, resources, communications, and even laws, and will have different metrics than if the solution is technology. Technologies usually have a significantly greater level of investment, including funding for development, prototyping, and testing, and thus require a more significant level of analysis to determine whether the technology is progressing toward deployment.

Regardless of the type of solution you are developing, both should be considered according to three factors:

1. the maturity of the solution being created
2. the investment capabilities of the team developing the solution
3. the adoption readiness of the accepting organization to incorporate the solution into their existing work

These categories are a simplified version of the more complex assessment necessary for technology solutions but still are a sound way to approach transitioning solutions into fully functioning capabilities.

FIGURE 8.2 WHEN TO MEASURE SOLUTION READINESS LEVELS

When to Measure Solution Readiness Levels

Source — Curate — Discover — Incubate — Transition

SOLUTION MATURITY LEVEL

INVESTMENT READINESS LEVEL

ADOPTION READINESS LEVEL

NON-TECHNOLOGY SOLUTIONS

Each of the steps (maturity, investment, and adoption) should be characterized by a simple assessment: a score of 1 means little to no maturity or capacity, and 3 being the most mature and capable state. For instance, say your solution is the development and deployment of a new human resources policy. You would measure the readiness of the solution to be fully developed, socialized, and integrated into existing policies with the following ratings.

Measuring the maturity of the human resources policy:

- 1 point assigned if the policy has not yet been written or reviewed, the appropriate draft and reviewing officials have not yet been secured, review of existing and dependent policies has not yet occurred, and the policy hasn't been socialized and approved by the appropriate officials.
- 2 points assigned if the policy is partially written and reviewed, the drafting and reviewing team have been selected, review of existing policies is taking place but not completed, and the draft policy is not yet in review.
- 3 points assigned if the draft policy is completed and reviewed.

Measuring the investment capabilities of the team developing the policy:

- 1 point assigned if an appropriate team to draft, review, and socialize the policy has not yet been assembled.
- 2 points assigned if an appropriate team to draft, review, and socialize the policy is partially assembled.
- 3 points assigned if an appropriate team to draft, review, and socialize the policy has been assembled.

Measuring the adoption readiness of the policy:

- 1 point assigned if the person responsible for human resources leadership is not yet informed or has not agreed to the policy inclusion, no human resources point of contact has been informed or included in the development team, and human resources policy hasn't been informed.
- 2 points assigned if leadership is agreeable, but the human resources team is not prepared or able to get the policy socialized, implemented, or promulgated.
- 3 points assigned if human resources, from its leadership to the implementor of policy, is on board with the proposed policy and ready to socialize, implement, and promulgate the policy.

TECHNOLOGY SOLUTIONS

To characterize the readiness of technology solutions developed in the pipeline to be transitioned into the broader organization, build on the concepts just considered (maturity, investment, and adoption) by measuring technology readiness level (TRL), investment readiness level (IRL), and adoption readiness level (ARL). TRL, IRL, and ARL are known industry standards with widely accepted and recognized levels.

FIGURE 8.3 THE INNOVATION PIPELINE TRANSITION DECISION SUPPORT TOOL

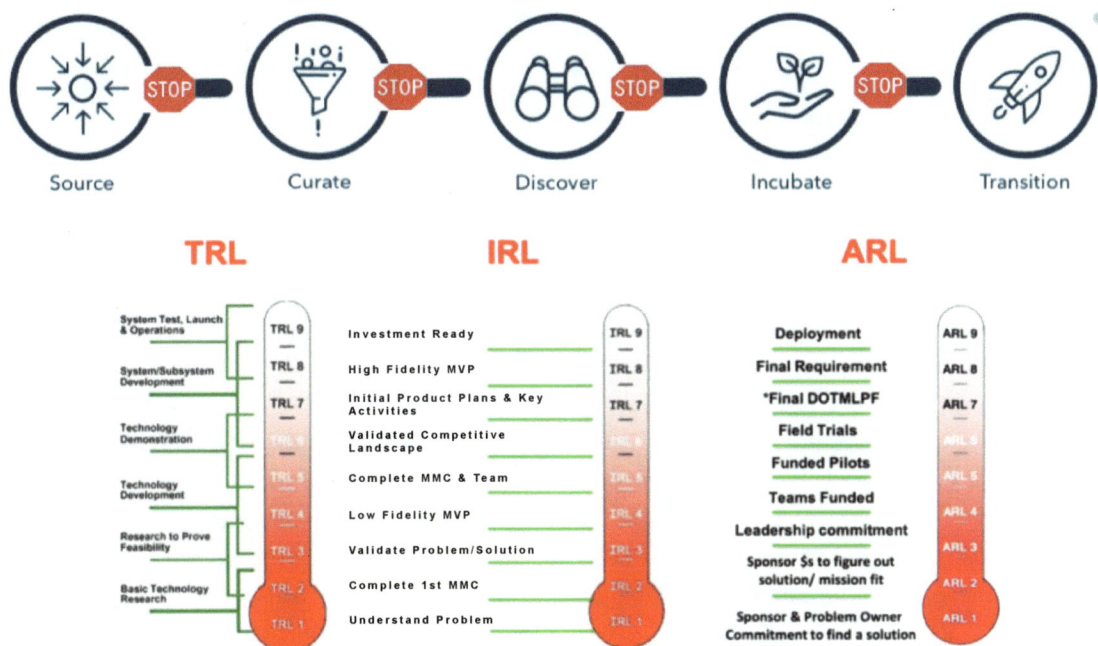

TRL, the technology readiness level, refers to the level of maturity of a technology solution in transitioning to a program of record and integrating the solution into existing portfolio of projects. Having a sufficient TRL maturity minimizes the risk to your agency in expending resources to realize the solution. TRL is determined by a combination of factors indicated by the IRL and the ARL. TRL, IRL, and ARL are measured on a scale from 1 to 9, with corresponding factors for each level, or gates to be met before preceding to the next level. Figure 8.3 illustrates the various gates for each level of TRL, ARL, and IRL and is primarily intended to evaluate the readiness of a technology solution for transition. But with some modification, this tool can be used to evaluate any type of solution, whether involving strategies, policies, processes, or communications.

IRL, the investment readiness level, refers to the maturity of the team and business processes— how ready are the aggregated staff to accept the workload that comes with executing the tasks necessary to incubate and transition solutions into existing programs, and how developed and reliable are the business processes that will enable the incubation and transitions. Obviously, with new teams and untested processes, more challenges will occur in the incubation and transition stages. But with time and through lessons learned, teams will unify in their actions, and processes will be ironed out. It is possible to scale the team and business process to bring an increasing level of effort and deliver an increasing number of solutions that are ready for transition.

ARL, the adoption readiness level, refers to the maturity, operational support available, aggregated skill sets of the team, and the ability of the end user to ingest and accept the transitioning solution into the normal course of business and existing programs and projects.

IRL and ARL can be measured to assess the maturity and readiness of a solution before proceeding (see Appendix L). If the solution is found to be not yet sufficiently mature to proceed from incubation into transition, you must determine the level of resources (development, staff time and attention, funding) required for it to continue to move through the Innovation Pipeline. Both IRL and ARL should be considered from a high-level perspective as soon as a solution is envisioned. If the solution investment costs are too high to realize a final product, or if the accepting program of record will never be ready to integrate such a solution into its normal work, the solution should be abandoned before additional time and resources are spent on it.

These metrics and the processes to craft them may seem a complex or even superfluous undertaking, but far from it—they will provide you the data you need to adjust your pipeline to maximize the results. There may be experts within your organization, perhaps an office, or even contractor support, who specialize in creating and monitoring performance metrics on a wide variety of programs. If needed, enlist their help in crafting the right metrics for your own Innovation Pipeline. You may be surprised in what the data reveal.

8.7 Communicating Your Innovation Pipeline

The information you have collected and maintained becomes irrelevant if it is not communicated on a regular basis. Your metrics should be communicated not only to your senior leadership and sponsor, but also to your action officers, team members, end users, and key partners so they understand your activities, successes, and challenges. Having each understand both what you are trying to achieve with your Innovation Pipeline and how you are achieving it is important. Create mechanisms to share your metrics with leadership,

stakeholders, and the broader workforce as well. These regular metrics communications will not only lead to greater buy-in of your stakeholders but also illustrate the successes achieved, so they can spread the good news. Your updates will also highlight where pipeline steps or activities may be falling behind in schedule or efficacy. This information can illustrate to them, with your gentle reminders, why and how your stakeholders and partners need to contribute to achieving your mutual goals.

Module 8 Key Takeaways

- Metrics should be used to inform your senior leadership and sponsor about your program performance and progress and to alert them to your innovation and mission successes.

- Each step of the Innovation Pipeline requires its own metrics to adequately assess its performance.

- It's critical to also measure the overall impact on mission your innovation efforts are having, rather than merely measuring the activities and outputs of innovation.

- Only through regular review of the pipeline can you identify gaps in the process and execute remedies to shore them up.

- Widely communicate metrics to your senior leadership and sponsor, action officers, team members, stakeholders, end users, and key partners so they understand your activities, successes, and challenges.

EXERCISE: CREATING METRICS TO MEASURE YOUR INNOVATION PIPELINE

This exercise will help you develop metrics for elements of each step of your Innovation Pipeline. Use the maturity/investment/adoption model for non-technology solutions, or the TRL=IRL+ARL model for technology solutions.

STEP	ELEMENT	METRICS
SOURCING		
	PIPELINE AND INFRASTRUCTURE	
	ACTIVITIES, METHODOLOGIES, AND TOOLS	
	DATA TRACKED	
	OPERATIONAL SUPPORT	
CURATION		
	PIPELINE AND INFRASTRUCTURE	
	ACTIVITIES, METHODOLOGIES, AND TOOLS	
	DATA TRACKED	
	OPERATIONAL SUPPORT	
DISCOVERY		
	PIPELINE AND INFRASTRUCTURE	
	ACTIVITIES, METHODOLOGIES, AND TOOLS	
	DATA TRACKED	
	OPERATIONAL SUPPORT	

STEP	ELEMENT	METRICS
INCUBATION		
	PIPELINE AND INFRASTRUCTURE	
	ACTIVITIES, METHODOLOGIES, AND TOOLS	
	DATA TRACKED	
	OPERATIONAL SUPPORT	
TRANSITION		
	PIPELINE AND INFRASTRUCTURE	
	ACTIVITIES, METHODOLOGIES, AND TOOLS	
	DATA TRACKED	
	OPERATIONAL SUPPORT	

Notes:

EXERCISE: INNOVATION PIPELINE SELF ASSESSMENT

This exercise will help you assess your Innovation Pipeline. Use it monthly to determine the relative health of each step of your pipeline.

INNOVATION PIPELINE SELF ASSESSMENT KEY

Strategy

- What's the goal for the Team
- What's the goal for Leadership

Pipeline & Infrastructure Process

Process
- What's the input and where does it come from?
- What's the output (deliverable product of this step)?

Team / Resources
- What team and what expertise is needed?
- What resources are required (funding, contracts, exceptions)

Operational Support

- Type of organizational support required (contracts, HR, Security)
- What leadership is required (resource/compliance decisions, firefighting etc)

Activities, Methodologies, Tools and Metrics

Activities and Methodologies
- What methodologies are used to perform this step
- Skills required and experiences needed

Tools and Skills
- Tools applied to collect insight
- Skills need to enable execution

Data and Assessments
- What metrics are used to measure throughput
- What vital signs (data) are used to check performance

SOURCE

Teams' goals are defined Score ☐	**Leaderships' goal is defined** Score ☐
Appropriate input is available Score ☐	**Output is generated to drive next step** Score ☐
Team & expertise is available Score ☐	**Resources are available** Score ☐
Organizational support is available Score ☐	**Leadership available & decisions points identified** Score ☐
Activities executed to generate output Score ☐	**Methodologies defined/used to guide discovery** Score ☐
Tools defined to collect insight Score ☐	**Training provide to develop execution skills** Score ☐
Metrics are defined to determine success Score ☐	**Data is collected to measure vital signs** Score ☐

1 – Exceptional. 2 – Adequate, requires constant oversight. 3 – Non-existent or not available

*Higher scores reflect increasing risk

*Total Score ☐

CURATE

Teams' goals are defined Score ☐	Leaderships' goal is defined Score ☐
Appropriate input is available Score ☐	Output is generated to drive next step Score ☐
Team & expertise is available Score ☐	Resources are available Score ☐
Organizational support is available Score ☐	Leadership available & decisions points identified Score ☐
Activities executed to generate output Score ☐	Methodologies defined/used to guide discovery Score ☐
Tools defined to collect insight Score ☐	Training provide to develop execution skills Score ☐
Metrics are defined to determine success Score ☐	Data is collected to measure vital signs Score ☐

1 – Exceptional. 2 – Adequate, requires constant oversight. 3 – Non-existent or not available

*Higher scores reflect increasing risk

*Total Score ☐

DISCOVER

Teams' goals are defined Score ☐	**Leaderships' goal is defined** Score ☐
Appropriate input is available Score ☐	**Output is generated to drive next step** Score ☐
Team & expertise is available Score ☐	**Resources are available** Score ☐
Organizational support is available Score ☐	**Leadership available & decisions points identified** Score ☐
Activities executed to generate output Score ☐	**Methodologies defined/used to guide discovery** Score ☐
Tools defined to collect insight Score ☐	**Training provide to develop execution skills** Score ☐
Metrics are defined to determine success Score ☐	**Data is collected to measure vital signs** Score ☐

1 – Exceptional. 2 – Adequate, requires constant oversight. 3 – Non-existent or not available

*Higher scores reflect increasing risk

*Total Score ☐

INCUBATE

Teams' goals are defined Score ☐	Leaderships' goal is defined Score ☐
Appropriate input is available Score ☐	Output is generated to drive next step Score ☐
Team & expertise is available Score ☐	Resources are available Score ☐
Organizational support is available Score ☐	Leadership available & decisions points identified Score ☐
Activities executed to generate output Score ☐	Methodologies defined/used to guide discovery Score ☐
Tools defined to collect insight Score ☐	Training provide to develop execution skills Score ☐
Metrics are defined to determine success Score ☐	Data is collected to measure vital signs Score ☐

1 – Exceptional. 2 – Adequate, requires constant oversight. 3 – Non-existent or not available

*Higher scores reflect increasing risk

*Total Score ☐

TRANSITION

Teams' goals are defined	Leaderships' goal is defined
Score ☐	Score ☐

Appropriate input is available	Output is generated to drive next step
Score ☐	Score ☐

Team & expertise is available	Resources are available
Score ☐	Score ☐

Organizational support is available	Leadership available & decisions points identified
Score ☐	Score ☐

Activities executed to generate output	Methodologies defined/used to guide discovery
Score ☐	Score ☐

Tools defined to collect insight	Training provide to develop execution skills
Score ☐	Score ☐

Metrics are defined to determine success	Data is collected to measure vital signs
Score ☐	Score ☐

1 – Exceptional. 2 – Adequate, requires constant oversight. 3 – Non-existent or not available

*Higher scores reflect increasing risk

*Total Score ☐

GLOSSARY

The following terms, used throughout this book to describe the Innovation Pipeline, are intended to give federal innovators a common language, process, and understanding.

Activities: The work that you and your innovation team and partners will do to realize your Innovation Pipeline, each of its five steps, and the problems and solutions emanating from it.

Beneficiaries/End Users/Customers: The people who will ultimately use and benefit from the solutions you and your innovation team create to solve your agency's tough problems; they may be critical infrastructure workers, law enforcement officials, human services providers, first responders, intelligence officers, or warfighters.

Components: The building blocks of an innovation organization, including people (senior support and innovation team); partnerships; contracting authorities and acquisition; funding; and agency support, which includes legal, security, IT, testing and development, strategy and policy, human resources, and congressional.

Curating: Step 2 of the Innovation Pipeline (along with prioritizing); the process of assessing problems to understand the true nature of the problems generated, looking for the root causes, and/or assessing the problem against agency or mission strategies, followed by the process of prioritizing the problems.

Discovering: Step 3 of the Innovation Pipeline; the process of developing and analyzing potential solutions more closely through research to create initial minimally viable products (MVPs).

Elements: There are five elements in each of the five steps that create the infrastructure of the Innovation Pipeline: process; activities (including inputs and outputs), methodologies, and tools; data; metrics; and operational support. These are described in Module 2 and Appendix A.

Factors: Criteria that a problem must meet to be considered worth pursuing:
- Desirable: is it wanted by the end user?
- Viable: is it supported politically?
- Feasible: is it possible?

Incubation: Step 4 of the Innovation Pipeline; the process of building or developing early versions of minimally viable products (MVPs) that are repeatable and scalable.

Infrastructure: The raw materials that fuel your Innovation Pipeline, which includes the five elements (process; activities/methodologies/tools; data; metrics; and operational support).

Innovation: Positive change in your organization; improving the outcomes of your organization by finding new ways to approach old tasks that are better, more efficient, faster, cheaper, or less painful. Innovation is anything new that helps your organization accomplish its mission, from small improvements to processes or policies to successful moon shots.

Innovation Pipeline: A disciplined, repeatable, and scalable means to introduce and manage disruptive innovation within your organization. It gathers problems your organization faces, whether emerging or persistent, identifies solutions to those problems, and provides a pathway for solution adoption.

Inputs and Outputs: The work that goes into and comes out of each step of the Innovation Pipeline. Outputs are not the same as outcomes or impacts.

Minimally Viable Product (MVP): A conceptual approach that allows you to test whether the product meets the needs of end users.

Outcomes: The results of the innovation activities of your Innovation Pipeline.

Partners: Anyone outside your innovation organization, your agency, or the federal government who can provide opportunities to expand and deliver on your innovation or pipeline goals. Partners can be other agency members, other federal agencies, military, intelligence community, law enforcement, homeland security, industry, academia, think tanks, nonprofits, state and local agencies, and international partners.

Prioritizing: The process of ranking problems, in 1 to n order, according to the agency's mission and strategic goals; part of step 2 of the Innovation Pipeline (along with curating).

Problems: The wide range of challenges your agency faces daily, which could be in agency strategy, policies, or processes, and which make work more difficult, complex, confusing, or frustrating for you and your colleagues.

Prototype: An initial version that allows you to test whether a product meets the needs of end users.

Solutions: Ways of remedying the problems you and your colleagues faces, which may include new or revised policies, processes, authorities, tools (such as playbooks), resources, communications, and even laws (although these require congressional action). Innovation solutions can solve challenges in any aspect of government work—operations, acquisition and contracting, funding, security, operations, performance management, and policy, to name a few.

Sourcing: Step 1 of the Innovation Pipeline; the process of discovering and collecting problems from a wide range of sources, both internal and external to your agency, to ultimately develop solutions to these problems.

Stakeholders: Individuals and organizations with a vested interest in your innovation activities; they include the senior leader, economic sponsors, end users and beneficiaries of your innovation efforts, action officers, technical experts (including acquisition, technology, programmatic, legislative, communications, and others), partners, and saboteurs.

Steps: There are five steps within the Innovation Pipeline: sourcing problems, curating problems, discovering problems, incubating solutions, and transitioning solutions.

Transitioning: Step 5 of the Innovation Pipeline; moving a mature technology or solution from prototype to integration into regular operations.

APPENDIX A: INNOVATION PIPELINE INFRASTRUCTURE

To build each of the five steps of the Innovation Pipeline (sourcing, curating, discovering, incubating, and transitioning), the following elements should be considered:

- *The pipeline and infrastructure processes to achieve the inputs and outputs of each step*
- *The activities (including inputs and outputs), methodologies, and tools to achieve each step*
- *The data you will track to indicate pipeline step robustness*
- *The metrics you will gather and analyze to illustrate pipeline performance*
- *The operational support you need to execute the activities, including funding, personnel, skill sets, contracting support, legal, security, and/or IT*

This appendix outlines what each element might consist of within each step. For more information regarding the inputs, outputs, and possible activities within each pipeline step, see Appendix B.

Step 1: Sourcing Problems

Pipeline and Infrastructure Processes

- Inputs to sourcing: Active sourcing efforts both internal and external to your organization to understand workforce pain points and end user needs
- Outputs to curation: Large pool of people, technology, ideas, and problems (with the pool continuously refreshed)

Activities, Methodologies, and Tools

- Activities: Sourcing problems, identifying wide range of problem sources
- Methodologies: Funnel, hackathons, crowd sourcing, Kickstarters, external partnerships, proxy generation, outreach services, extraction workshops, H4X
- Tools: Osterwalder portfolio management, innovation pipeline model, input/output ratio, funnel metrics, problem sourcing canvas

Data

- Number and diversity of independent sources (tech, people, problems, and ideas) across the 3 horizons of potential innovation
- Number of active engagements from the pool that remain engaged in follow-on steps (e.g., number of innovators and entrepreneurs moving into curation)
- Number of vetted problems accepted into curation

Metrics

- Number of active internal and external sourcing programs
- Ratio of new sources netted from each event to those actually engaged in other parts of the pipeline over time (passive vs. active connections)
- Ratio of entities sourced to entities accepted into next phase (1:1 ratio indicates a weak sourcing mechanism; 4:1 is preferable)

Operational Support

- Organizational support: Contracts, HR, security, engineering, and R&D liaisons with familiarity in alternative acquisition processes
- Leadership support: Prioritize current and future problems for the innovation team; provide the support to allow rapid and fast-track internal and external sourcing of tech, problems, and people by providing parallel processes for security, contracting, HR, finance, policy, and engineering
- Skills: Active and aggressive "ecosystem architects" with knowledge of the mission space and strong skills in communicating, connecting, and building ecosystems around mission sets; internal and external

sourcing programs
- Skills/experiences to perform sourcing: Aggressive connector, team/coalition builder, connection to senior leadership, organizational silo breaker
- Skills for execution: Aggressive ecosystem development team, H4X, Lean
- Resources:
  - Full-time and contract sourcing team
  - Possible physical space
  - Contracting, finance and acquisition, legal, and security liaisons
  - Resources for travel and to host sourcing events (e.g., hackathons, sprints)

Step 2: Curating Problems

Pipeline and Infrastructure Processes
- Inputs from sourcing: Healthy and diverse pool of ideas, problems, technology, and innovators from active internal and external sourcing programs
- Outputs to discovery: Prioritized portfolio of curated problems; concept sketch for how the problem presents itself, initial tech and expert ecosystem map, problem sponsor and champion for each problem
- Innovation team expertise needed: Problem curation team, technology analysis, ecosystem architects
- Resources: Full-time curation team, physical space, contracting, financing, legal, and security liaisons; funding for travel; organizational OK for curation team to spend time on problems/tech in the pipeline, teams into the pipeline

Activities, Methodologies, and Tools
- Activities: Active outreach to find problems and sponsors, problem curation workshops, technology exploration
- Methodologies: Problem curation, Concept of Operations (CONOPs) development, MVP development, Mission Model Canvas (MMC), portfolio map, investment readiness level (IRL)/technology readiness level (TRL)/adoption readiness level (ARL)
- Tools: Problem curation workbook, petal diagrams, Value Proposition Canvas (VPC), Collaboration Map

Data
- Number of beneficiary, innovator, entrepreneur, and tech expert interviews conducted to validate problems and ideas
- Diversity of innovators, entrepreneurs, and experts engaged in validation

Metrics
- Ratio of problems/new concepts curated vs. those accepted into discovery (1:1 reflects a weak pool; 4:1 is closer to historical norms from REF and H4D)
- Ratio of problems/new concepts spread across Alex Osterwalder's portfolio map vs. 3 horizons
- Initial TRL/IRL and ARL established
- Quality of teams in discovery: how many meet minimum standard and remain intact?

Operational Support
- Organizational support: Contracts, HR, security, engineering and R&D liaisons with authority for sourcing exceptions
- Leadership support: Top-level agreement for fast-track sourcing, committed funding, written exceptions for security, contracting, policy, legal for innovation sourcing
- Skills and experiences: Problem curation, talking to humans, interviewing, Lean, technology assessment, design thinking, MVP development, iterative development

Step 3: Discovering Solutions

Pipeline and Infrastructure Processes
- Inputs from curation: Prioritized portfolio of curated problems; for each problem, concept sketch for how the problem presents itself, initial tech and expert ecosystem map, problem sponsor and champion
- Outputs to incubation: Validated MVPs, test data, and a pathway to deliver a solution; teams with the potential to deliver; early adopters/first customers identified

Activities, Methodologies, and Tools
- Activities: Hacking for Defense, I-Corps, Exploration workshops, discovery workshops, product jam/experimentation workshop
- Methodologies: Lean Startup, MVP development, Mission Model Canvas (MMC), Business Model Canvas (BMC), portfolio management
- Tools: Mission Model Canvas (MMC), Business Model Canvas (BMC), innovation portfolio map, investment decision support tools (IRL, TRL, ARL), funnel metrics, workflow maps, user journey maps, HMW statements

Metrics
- Ratio of teams entering discovery to those moving on to incubation (1:1 ratio is flat, historical norm from venture due diligence; H4D and REF is ~4:1)
- TRL, IRL, and ARL established as part of decision to move forward into incubation
- Ratio of teams in discovery spread across Alex Osterwalder's portfolio map vs. 3 horizons
- Quality of team transitioning to incubation (focused on left side of MMC)

Data
- Number of hypothesis and MVPs generated
- Number of team pivots
- Number and diversity of interviews conducted
- TRL, IRL, and ARL at completion of discovery
- Number of external partners and internal parts of organization engaged

Operational Support
- Contracts, HR, security, engineering, and R&D liaisons with authority for discovery and MVPs
- Understanding how to "get to yes" from those groups
- Unfettered access to potential beneficiaries
- Coaches and mentors to support teams in discovery
- Top-level agreement for fast track MVPs
- Funding for teams in the discovery process (travel, prototyping, stipends, pay)
- Written exceptions for security, contracting, policy, legal for innovation sourcing
- Designated/trained organizational POCs in contracting, HR, resource management
- Firefighting board of organizational leaders capable of reducing barriers for innovation teams
- Innovation team expertise needed: Lean/I-Corps instructors, internal entrepreneurs recruited to teams to build agency buy-in and coalition
- Expertise for the team in the pipeline: Hypothesis generation, MVP development, MVP testing development, Interviewing techniques, data capture
- Resources: Full-time innovation team, physical space, contracting, financing, legal and security liaisons; funding for travel; organizational OK for innovators to spend time on problems/tech in the pipeline, teams into the pipeline; other organizations bought into (1) fast-track process, (2) adoption of output
- Skills and experiences: Innovation teams need innovators + entrepreneurs; pipeline leadership team needs to build agency buy-in and coalition; internal and external entrepreneurs recruited to teams; prototyping ability

Step 4: Incubating Solutions

Pipeline and Infrastructure Processes
- Inputs from discovery: Validated MVPs and test data and a pathway to deliver a solution; teams with the potential to deliver.
- Early adopters/first customer identified
- Outputs to transitioning: Investible entity with validated IRL, TRL, and ARL

Activities, Methodologies, and Tools
- Methodologies: MVPs, MMC, active coaching and mentoring, transition plans, scale and deployment plans
- Tools: MMC, IRL, TRL, ARL, funnel metrics

Data
- Number and ratio of MVPs moving to prototype development
- Size/scale of initial and subsequent user pools gained during incubation
- Funding committed to team during incubation
- Number and amount of follow-on investment, grants, and government contracts received
- Number of other organizations engaged

Metrics
- Ratio of teams in incubation to those gaining follow-on investment (for H1 teams, maybe 2:1, H2 teams 4:1, H3 teams 10:1)
- Change in TRL, IRL, and ARL of teams throughout incubation and at departure to transition
- Condensation: Number of projects in discovery combined into one effort moving forward to incubation

Operational Support
- Innovation team expertise needed: Domain expert coaches and mentors, pipeline leadership to build agency buy-in and coalition; understanding the politics of transition
- Skills/experiences to perform incubation: Innovation teams need innovators + entrepreneurs + developers; pipeline leadership team continues to build agency buy-in and coalition; recruit developers to teams in pipeline
- Skills for execution: Investment due diligence, government contracts/grants management; prototyping, agile development, Scrum, IP assignment, partnership building, business development
- Recruit developers to teams in pipeline, physical space, contracting, financing, legal and security liaisons.
- Funding for travel and funding for teams; organizational OK for innovators to spend full-time on problems/tech in the pipeline.
- Other organizations bought into (1) fast-track process, (2) adoption of output
- Organizational support: Contracts, HR, security, engineering, and R&D liaisons with authority for discovery and MVPs; understanding how to "get to yes" from those groups; coaches and mentors
- Written agreement for how incubation moves to transition from contracting, security, legal, engineering, etc.
- Funding for teams; written exceptions for security, contracting, policy, legal for innovation sourcing
- Firefighting board of organizational leaders capable of reducing barriers for innovation teams
- Prioritization for testing and evaluation

Step 5: Transitioning Solutions

Pipeline and Infrastructure Processes
- Inputs from incubation: Investible entity with validated IRL, TRL, and ARL
- Outputs to the agency: A scalable solution that is delivered in time to have an impact

Activities, Methodologies, and Tools
- Methodologies: Refactoring, organizational change management, sustainment packaging, training development, Kaizen for continuous improvement (Toyota's engineering way)
- Tools: User surveys, adoptions surveys, localization tools (solution performance at different units, bases, etc.)

Data
- Realized beneficiary value (impact on original problem)
- IRL, TRL, and ARL at transition to program of record (POR)
- Scaled implementation data (user drop-off/pain points/patches or modifications required)

Metrics
- Ratio of teams receiving initial investment leaving incubation to those receiving follow-on investment (different ratios for H1, H2, and H3)
- Ratio of teams in transition to those accepted in POR or theater sustainment (different ratios for H1, H2, and H3)
- Average time spent in transition (shorter for H1; longer for H3)

Operational Support
- Contracts, HR, security, engineering and R&D liaisons with authority for prototype development, testing, and evaluations
- Access to users; understanding how to "get to yes" from those groups; coaches and mentors
- Innovation team expertise: At this step oversight responsibility should move from the the innovation team to a transition team capable of refactoring the solution to deliver at scale
- Skills/experiences: Agile, Scrum, deployment planning, training development, integration, supply chain management
- Skills for execution: Transition management, budgeting, experimentation design, supply chain development, POR management, POM planning
- Funds for testing, advanced prototyping, and access to facilities
- Funds for training, sustainment for 1 year to support the transition of a prototype into a POR
- Augment the innovation team with members of the organizational transition team
- Written agreement for how incubation moves to transition from contracting, security, legal, engineering, etc.
- Funding for teams; written exceptions for security, contracting, policy, legal for innovation sourcing
- Firefighting board of organizational leaders capable of reducing barriers for scaling teams
- Prioritization for testing, evaluation, and forward deployment

APPENDIX B: INNOVATION PIPELINE INPUTS, ACTIVITIES, AND OUTPUTS

To build upon the elements presented in Appendix A, this appendix captures the inputs, activities, and outputs for each of the five steps of the Innovation Pipeline. It is meant to provide guidance as you build, implement, and refine your own Innovation Pipeline.

- *Inputs are information and resources needed for each step.*
- *Activities are potential actions to be performed at each phase.*
- *Outputs are the information, documents, and knowledge that should result from completion of the phase.*

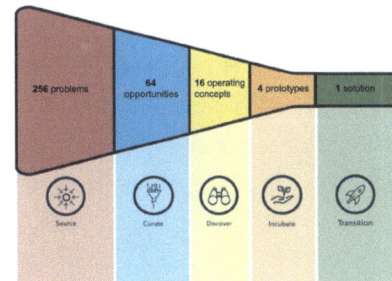

This document is meant to be a guide, not a strict prescription. If any of the inputs/activities/outputs are not applicable, feel free to move on to the next step, but each will reduce the risk in successfully transitioning a solution.

Step 1: Source: Where are people struggling? What is of interest to my organization?

Sourcing involves building networks around interest areas and collecting not only problems but ideas, facts, opportunities, existing solutions (and their limitations), end users with problems, and potential solution owners. Note that problems are one element of sourcing; you should source contacts, technologies, capabilities, and companies and relate them in clusters. We often talk of a "sourcing fusion cell" so that this information, which can be dynamic, is available and loosely connected/linked.

Inputs
- Problems: discrete challenges
- Problem domains: portfolios of discrete challenges
- Strategic guidance (e.g., unmanned campaign, key operational problems, intelligence autonomous systems strategy)
- Ideas: prospective technologies and concepts sourced from end users and creators
- Solutions: existing technology, ongoing R&D, parallel processes
- Stakeholders
    - Partners
    - Funders
    - Investors
    - Companies, small businesses
    - Requirements owner/sponsor
- Gaps: gaps in knowledge, technology, capabilities, requirements

Activities
- Organize workshops: immerse into the problem domain, empathize and assess domain context. Collect a wide range of different problems, ideas, and stakeholders to organize/synthesize into clusters (problem sourcing/extraction workshop)
- Scan the domain: get an initial understanding of the market, available technologies, and relevant people
- Map stakeholders (version 1.0): understand the domain, pain points, who is relevant, who is not, who are potential saboteurs, and where to get inspiration/information
- Organize thinking: gathering/prioritizing assumptions, constraints, needs (requirements, small "r")

- Problem domain/map to better contextualize why the problem exists and how it exists
- Problem statement document(s) to detail the problem and relevant background context: Synthesizes what is known and identifies knowledge gaps between the current state and the desired future state
- Curated list of contacts: Individuals who can contribute problems, people, funding, and ideas
- Initial stakeholder map/personas to understand and analyze who is involved, and how the individuals, organizations, and resources may be connected

Step 2: Curate: Is the problem important enough to justify further investment?

Curation takes problem areas/problem statements and digs deeper. Depending on the nature of the problem, this step is about assessing the real problem—looking for the root cause—and/or the strategy. This phase requires more time, especially if the problem is of a technical nature, and likely involves not just new technical developments but also CONOPs ideation. This phase is important for prioritizing resources.
- Find out why there is a problem, who is specifically affected, and how it might have manifested within the organization.
- Rigorously assess and prioritize focus areas by opportunity cost. Often problems can be solved at the local level, by connecting to the right entities (warfare centers), or by coaching on funding (local organizations have funding they don't know about).

Inputs
- Outputs from sourcing phase (problem statements, stakeholder map(s), list of potential capabilities/ technologies/companies to consider, list of contacts)

Activities
- Conduct beneficiary interviews: Validate understanding of problems, deconstruct problems, map problems against operational needs, and empathize with the perspective of the beneficiary (the person struggling with the problem directly). Beneficiaries have roles that directly interface with the problem being observed; beneficiaries are not agencies, subdivisions, or indirectly tangential to the problem.
- Conduct market/domain research: Sufficiently understand the broad trends of a market or domain and relevant examples that align to your problem; acquire enough data to form an informed opinion on a subject. Look at the commercial market and emerging technology markets to review not just technologies but associated business models.
- Prioritize your efforts: Develop evaluation/prioritization criteria. Conduct an impact/effort exercise. Estimate the best trade-off of time or effort for value or urgency to your organization. Rank in order (do NOT just categorize into priority 1 or 2 or 3, as everything likely will end up as priority 1). Force initial trade-offs.
- Remap your stakeholders: Apply new data to visualize the relevant people to your problem. Include non-naval entities. Who shares your pain? As part of the stakeholder diagram, identify who would be potential partners for:
  - Funding
  - Technical diligence
  - Experimentation
  - Program framework and scaling

Outputs
- Detailed Problem Statement with:
  - Single problem owner identified (ideally a single name): Who cares and who is accountable?
  - Operational description/mission area analysis: Why is this a problem?
  - Assumptions: What conditions/aspects are we taking for granted?
  - Constraints, unavoidable requirements around key problems: What are we limited by?
  - Relevant resources: What help/support do we have?

- Plotted on Mission Model Canvas (v1)
- List of prioritized problems on impact-to-effort map and approaches to perform discovery (who will you talk to and why?) for each problem on the prioritized list (this can also filter for priority)
- Preliminary market/problem domain research list of references (e.g., if machine learning is a potential solution for a problem; aggregated references where it has been used in industry to solve similar problems)
- Short list of companies or technologies that may have solutions to the problem space
- Short list of technology gaps to inform research that can solve the problem set and its estimated time to see results
- Preliminary list of scaling/transition stakeholders and pathways, including warfare development and operational units, not just program offices; should include non-naval and congressional stakeholders
    - Purpose: To prepare for those prioritized problem domains with potential solutions that go into discovery. Initial considerations should be generated and advanced while the solution is being prototyped.
- Rejected problems with reasons for their rejection (e.g., no problem owner, lower priority, lack of clarity, refinement). This step is important to note why problems were rejected and sent back a phase. Reasoning may become relevant to inform other phases or outside stakeholders.

Step 3: Discover: What's the cheapest fastest test I can perform to validate (or invalidate) my assumptions? Do the data indicate we validated both the problem and a basic solution?

Discover takes potential MVPs and tests hypotheses and assumptions to assess operational, market, and technology to inform later development of the solution. Is the solution viable? Is it usable before investing too much? If a solution is not viable, pivot. Is it sponsored? If a solution is not sponsored, start exploring sponsors. Understand key reasons, validate or invalidate hypotheses, and think of the adoption cycle (leverage early adopter archetypes but do NOT assume they represent a critical mass for scaling).

Inputs
- Outputs from curation (prioritized problems, a detailed problem statements, initial domain research)
- Organized list of hypotheses (5–8) from the identified assumptions about each solution to work against the problem area

Activities
- "How Might We" (HMW) statements: Rephrase known problems as a question beginning with "How Might We"; this helps create a space for creative thinking of "out-of-the-box" solutions, to pair or research more potential solutions; solutions may not be technical, or exquisite
- Organize an ask the experts call: Engage and ask questions of outside expert perspectives
- Organize an exploration workshop: Series of rapid-fire calls with solution providers (industry, public) to vet potential solution ideas found elsewhere in the market or domain
- Organize a design sprint: Typically a 5-day sprint, to validate ideas and build and test an MVP
- Solicit user centered preview of potential training needs: Start collecting potential training needs; these can inform constraints on potential solutions
- Downselect solution ideas via an impact effort map (introduced in curate step)
- Organize another design sprint (3–5 consecutive day sequestered activity) to address solution ideas; may include ideation around CONOPs, integration strategy, and potential approaches to acquisitions
- Hold an additional design sprint to develop funding pitch/storytelling
- Update the Mission Model Canvas (MMC): Map with a potential solution to visualize and communicate the business model for mission-driven organizations; this allows for the search of unknowns and framing of hypotheses
    - Iteratively update with each MVP cycle
- Minimum Viable Product Development (three iterations is common): Develop the basic capabilities/ features for use to collect user feedback; incorporate feedback in following iterations until assumptions are all tested and users are satisfied. See above for emphasis on viable.

- Investment or budget request pitch: Ensure enough funding to sustain the building of prototypes (for the Integration step, where experimentation starts in earnest)
  - While not needed for the pitch, research should be done under the assumption that the prototype is to be scaled. What training and sustainment considerations are needed?

Outputs
- HMW statements
- Winning solution sketches with notes of what is important about the solution idea (may be a composite of solutions reviewed during curation)
- Mission Model Canvas v.2 with list of validated, invalidated hypotheses
  - List of potential transition partners
  - Stakeholder map
  - Tested MVPs with lessons learned (lessons learned are critical to collect)
  - Risks identified (can be mitigated through MVP tests, or note untested hypotheses that do not have time to be tested but recommend the team proceeds)
  - Invalidated hypotheses (rejected approaches, REF attrition: 115/360 = 32%)
- Initial CONOPs paired with solution MVPs
- Target POR or two to three ideas on an acquisition pathway
- Initial TRL, ARL, IRL assessment
  - IRL: Investment readiness level. A rating similar to TRL but focused on the amount of learning and validation captured in a solution/team's MMC
  - ARL: Adoption readiness level. A rating similar to TRL but focused on level of buy-in from key stakeholders
- Pitch: A presentation outlining the high-level solution to convince key stakeholders that this is a solution worth investing in
  - Include initial TRL, IRL, ARL assessment
  - Include MMC iterations, hypotheses validated/invalidated
  - End user communities involved
  - Target acquisition program
  - Integration strategy/ approach
  - Proposed key performance requirements
  - Initial contracting strategy elements with pros/cons (COCO/SAAS)
  - Proposed exit criteria from integration to transition
  - Budget with ROM and 20% up/down sensitivity analysis
  - High-level draft tech transition agreement (bullet points)
- Initial training needs: What talent is needed in the end user communities (e.g., today there is not enough data science or AI understanding)
- Rejected problems/solutions: Only one in four should move to incubation (be honest; do not combine solutions just to get them through the phase)

Step 4: Incubate: Are our early solutions scalable? What needs to change? Is the market ready? Is the industrial base robust?
Build early versions of the solution. (This is the stage where larger amounts will be spent. Discovery should provide ample justification to enter this phase. Formal gate review recommended.)

Inputs
- Outputs from discovery
- Gate review approving entry into incubation: Where MVPs are now prototypes and we move into experimentation (akin to an ACAT I Milestone A decision)
- Funding: This is the phase where a greater amount of funding is spent.

Activities

- Rapid prototyping: MVPs become prototypes; quickly build, test, iterate solutions; additional emphasis on usability
- Usability testing: User centered design—U/I iterations—to ensure solutions are not just engineering prototypes; significantly improves safety and reduction in cost of training; includes stakeholders who need to fix/sustain the solution
- Experimentation/experiments: Disciplined experimentation objectives with documented learning; business/operational experimentation objectives should be included
- Demonstration events: Somewhere where you display the culmination of the experimentation. When/where do you show what you've incubated?
- Discussions with funders/investors: Maintain alignment and communications
- Draft integration strategy and plan (systems of systems concepts)
  - Includes security and authority to operate
  - Includes software factory setup and alignment
- Draft training development: Ensure that end users can correctly use the solution
- Draft scaling plan: Enable reasonable scaling up of the solution
  - Ensure software factory available
- Draft CONOPs (v2)/playbook: How to use prototype to highlight the increased maturity of the solution
- Draft manufacturing and sustainment evaluation: Irrespective of whether a hardware or a software or hybrid solution, ensure solution can be consistently and reliably produced
- Draft REF 10-liner (a BMNT simplified requirements definition document): High-level think-through of the acquisitions process

Outputs

- Upgraded/documented prototype
- Investment pitch update: With gate review to exit phase
  - TRL, IRL, ARL (and initial integration readiness level, manufacturing readiness level assessment)
  - Annual PE funding levels committed to the program
  - Transition FY
  - Target POR draft CONOPs
  - Signed technology transition agreement with gaps and funding to plug gaps identified
  - REF 10-liner
  - Acquisitions plan
- Draft transition plans
  - Draft manufacturability assessment/manufacturing readiness level (MRL)
  - Draft scale and deployment plan
- Lessons learned from experimentation
  - Rejected solutions
  - Documented feedback from demonstration events
  - Documented feedback on funding/investment
- Pilot dependent on type of solution

Step 5: Transition Part I: What do we need to scale our solution?
Integrate and scale the mature solution.

Inputs

- Outputs from incubation phase I
- Scalable, validated solution with sustainment and upgrade requirements and funding outlined
- Funding: Investors who will fund scale (PEO, POM, etc.)
- Technology transition agreement (TTA)

Activities
- Finalize tech transition agreement
- Agreed-upon adoption plan: Keep stakeholders accountable
- Refactoring: Ensure capabilities are increased without any impact on existing capabilities
- Certifications: Confirm that capabilities are up to code and safe for use
- Finalize the manufacturing process (where relevant): Ensure the solution can be consistently and reliably produced
- CONOPs for sustainability
  - Software, AI, data sustainment included
- Finalize a training regimen: Ensure personnel will be sufficiently trained on the new capability
- Deploy the solution: Deliver capabilities to the fleet

Outputs
- Fieldable/fielded capabilities
- Training plan
- Deployment plan
- Sustainment plan
- Lessons learned along the way

Transition Part II: What do we need to do to sustain this solution?
Scale and sustain the mature solution.

Inputs
- Outputs from incubation
- Lessons learned (from transition part I and throughout the process)
- Transition partners

Activities
- Finalize contracting strategy
- Finalize/update budget requirements
- Finalize/update target POR; target warfighting communities involved
  - Which units receive and deploy first?
- Finalize training regimen: Continued successful utilization and implementation of the solution
- Finalize sustainment plan: Ensure continued competition and cost control while meeting end user mission requirements
- Finalize scaling plan: Enable production and deployment ramp up and scaling

Outputs
- Monitoring/sustainment plan
- Training regimen
- Scaling plan; scalable solution
- Budget defined and validated for scaling, training, deployment, and sustainment
- Scaled solution
- Rejected solutions that cannot scale (not high-priority, too expensive)

APPENDIX C: PROBLEM SOURCING AND GOOD PROBLEM OWNERS

This appendix provides insight into step 1 of the Innovation Pipeline, sourcing, and describes how to source problems and identifying the right kind of problem owners.

Problem Owner Characteristics

Problem owners are an integral component of the sourcing step. They take ownership of a problem and are deeply invested in finding a solution. Often, they have experience within the problem domain. Below, we highlight three criteria of a good problem owner based on our experience.

Autonomy

Successful problem owners are able to set their own priorities and juggle multiple responsibilities. Although problem discovery may be an initial effort in the Innovation Pipeline, problem owners are responsible for the solution. Therefore, must be highly committed to realizing and operationalizing the solution. Most of the real work comes after problem discovery and solution creation. The problem owner should be comfortable leading a team of people, some of whom may come from outside of their department.

Willingness to operate in a minimum viable framework

Great problem owners are willing to operate in the "minimum viable" framework, meaning they try to spend the least amount of money to learn the most information. This could mean settling for an 80% solution to deliver an urgent need. They will not be tempted to overengineer and perfect systems, delaying a product or process that can already alleviate the problem at hand.

Project management experience

Successful problem owners accurately anticipate the time and resource commitments that prototype development demands, whether technical, policy, communications, or other solutions. Problem owners should understand project management, funding cycles, and how to navigate the existing bureaucratic hoops in order to make a project actionable.

Finding Problem Owners

There are several ways to find good problem owners:

Approach 1: Participants bring their own problems

Identify four or five individuals who you think might be valuable early adopters—those who are keen to learn more about innovation and champion it among their colleagues. Tasking these individuals at least a week in advance of a workshop or problem curation call to allow them to thoughtfully identify a problem, consider pain points, and select appropriate end users. They may also spend time thinking about the right cross-functional team to work on the problem, which encourages a deeper exploration of the problem.

Approach 2: Command or organization submits command priority problems

Alternatively, the command can assign participants to problems that align with command priorities. Ideally, selected participants are matched to problems that align with the domains in which they work. Active engagement in the problem area will ensure that the team is well situated to continue their work after a workshop concludes.

Approach 3: Leadership provides problems they know exist

Usually, organizational leadership is aware of ways in which their organization needs to change in order to be more effective. Their problems should be taken seriously and considered.

End user interviews are a central part of a workshop. Problem owners should schedule interviews with end users as soon as a problem area is identified, as it is often difficult to identify, contact, and interview end users on short notice. Sometimes, participants may not work directly with end users in their usual roles and may need guidance in identifying or getting in touch with beneficiaries.

Sample Problem Statements

- The Joint Operations Center Staff needs a cohesive process for integrating and analyzing information from local partners in order to make the best operational decisions.
- Infantry units and radio operators need a way to practice identifying and responding to electromagnetic spectrum jamming in order to remain effective in communication compromised environments.
- Watchstanders need a way to automatically identify different watercraft from varying camera images in order to more accurately advise the ship's navigation.

APPENDIX D: CREATING "HOW MIGHT WE" STATEMENTS

This appendix supports step 2, curate, with guidelines for creating "How Might We" statements, which help frame organizational problems in a way that enables potential solutions for these problems.

PURPOSE
"How Might We" (HMW) statements are tools to frame problem statements in a way that helps users standardize the language and consider possible solutions for their challenges.

WHEN TO USE
Consider using HMW statements after identifying a specific challenge affecting the relevant target beneficiary, the entity that stands to gain from solving the pain point.

METHOD
1. Examine and deconstruct the existing problem statement
    a) Identify the **pain point**
    b) Identify the **beneficiary**
    c) Identify a **root cause of the pain point** (ideally one common across problem owners)
2. Draft a HMW statement using the following structure:
    a) Start with **How might we**
    b) Insert a **placeholder verb** that invokes change
    c) Insert the chosen **root cause**
    d) Insert **"to"** followed by the **pain point**
    e) Insert **"for"** followed by the **beneficiary**

How might we + change + root cause + to + pain point + for + beneficiary

3. Clean up and revise the statement for public discussion and interviews with problem owners.

EXAMPLE
"Our biggest thing that's not working is that we can't make rotors fast enough for our customers."

1. Examine and deconstruct problem statement and problem

Our biggest thing that's not working is that we can't **make rotors fast enough** for **our customers**. Several of our interviewees believe that **the manufacturing process** is part of the problem.

2. Draft initial HMW statement

How might we change **the manufacturing process** to **make rotors fast enough** for **our customers**?

3. Clean up and revise the HMW statement

How might we restructure our **manufacturing process** to meet **customer demand of rotors**?

This appendix supports steps 1 (source), 2 (curate), and 3 (discover) of the Innovation Pipeline with guidelines on how to maximize the results of interviewing stakeholders to better understand their needs and pain points.

10 INTERVIEWING TIPS TO REMEMBER

DOs / DON'Ts

#	DOs	DON'Ts
1	Go in prepared. Know your goals and questions ahead of time.	Don't have an endless list of questions.
2	Be smart about who you target. Work from your hypotheses on market and early adopters.	Don't take a shotgun approach, talking to anyone with a pulse.
3	Talk to one person at a time. If you bring a note taker, they should remain quiet.	Don't do focus groups.
4	Prepare yourself to hear things you don't want to hear.	Don't let your excitement and optimism bias what you hear.
5	Get stories on past behavior.	Don't ask people to speculate (i.e. "would you pay for X?")
6	Ask for advice.	Don't pitch unless you actually try to close for real money.
7	Listen. 95% of the conversation should be them talking.	Don't talk so much, and don't be afraid of silences. Let them think.
8	Follow your nose and drill down when something of interest comes up.	Don't feel like you have to rigidly stick to a script.
9	At the end of the interview, ask for introductions to more people to speak with.	Don't leave empty handed if you can help it.
10	Look for patterns and use judgement.	Don't take any one conversation literally.

#talkingtohumans
talkingtohumans.com

APPENDIX F: INTERVIEW NOTES TEMPLATE

This appendix maximizes interview productivity during steps 1, 2, and 3 of the pipeline. The template provided here can aid in gathering and tracking information to better understand the needs of your problem stakeholders. Interviews should be conducted according to problem domain areas or to address specific problems captured to understand the most relevant customer issues and needs for each problem or domain.

Before the Interview
- Write interview questions using the "How Might We" model (Appendix D)
- Pre-determine possible tags for the notes, for example:
  - Project type
  - Pain points
  - What they like
  - Referrals
  - Customer-determined data type
  - Answers to specific questions
- Create an interview tracking spreadsheet to track interviewee responses by each question, looking for patterns and commonalities or differences between the various types of interviewees

During the Interview
- A scribe takes interview notes, while the lead asks questions
- Add comments to the interviews with the pre-determined tags, which will identify important information in the future without having to re-read every interview
- Create new tags with common patterns you see in answers to each question; link the person's name from your interview notes

After the Interview
- Send a thank you email to each interviewee
- Tag all previous notes with any new tags you created
- Copy biographical and bold responses to a master interview spreadsheet

Data Analysis
- Read and understand each interviewee responses and general gist
- Compare answers to the same question among interviewees to capture the most important insights from each question
- Highlight the most important findings (stakeholder challenges and needs) for the problem. Think about these issues as you analyze the responses:
  - Should we be asking different questions?
  - Are the questions we ask giving us the answers we are looking for?
  - How are people answering the questions?
  - Which answers are repeated, and by whom?
  - What insights are we gathering as we interview more people?
  - When should we ask a next-level question once a hypothesis has been validated?
  - Do we want to solve this?
  - Is this a problem worth exploring?
  - Does the organization support solving this?

INTERVIEW NOTES TEMPLATE

Name:

Title/Role:

Organization:

Date of Interview:

Contact information:

Lead:

Scribe:

Recording:

Critical Questions

Key Takeaways

Additional Notes

Next Steps

INTERVIEW QUESTIONS TEMPLATE

List the archetype (senior leader, economic buyer, campaign sponsor, problem sponsor, campaign action officer, problem action officer, end user) and questions to ask during the interview.

Senior Leader

Q1.

Q2.

Q3.

Economic Buyer

Q1.

Q2.

Q3.

Problem Sponsor

Q1.

Q2.

Q3.

APPENDIX G: CONDUCTING REMOTE INTERVIEWS

This appendix, supporting steps 1, 2, and 3 of the pipeline, provides guidelines for conducting interviews over the phone, via Zoom, or via other video teleconference capabilities.

Prepare
- Read through any info you have about the person and problem prior to the call
- Write out questions you have about the problem; if you have only vague information, write broad questions
- Write out questions that will help you gather the three to four data points you need to meet the goals of the interview

Execute
- Record the calls so you have something to reference
    - Tip: Many conferencing services have transcription functionality
- Use the list of questions you wrote and take notes under each relevant question
    - Write down only what will help jog your memory about the call
    - If you come up with a new question while your interviewee is talking, jot it down so you don't lose track of it
    - Once they're done speaking, follow up: "You said something that I want to pull the thread on…"
- Learn, don't relate: Remain curious about the problem in terms of what is interesting for the organization to solve, not what is interesting to you
- Check off the critical data points as you gather them

Analyze
- As soon as possible after the conversation, take 15 minutes to review and clean your notes
    - This may mean rewriting them; aim for a clear narrative between the question asked and the answer given
    - Highlight anything interesting or salient you see related to the critical data you collected; you could add a comment and tag it with "beneficiary," "pain point," etc.
    - Highlight anything you don't know
    - Revisit your transcript in case you missed anything
- Tag others who were on the call with you to fill in specific things you don't remember
    - Don't fill in the blanks with your own research or experience
- Link your recording and/or transcription directly into these cleaned notes
- Share the notes with anyone who needs to contribute or stay informed

CONDUCTING REMOTE INTERVIEWS[5]
Adapted from Tom Uhlhorn

Customer research is a double-edged sword. On the good side, it informs the organization about what is valuable to their users; on the bad side, when user research is not accurate, it fills businesses with a false sense of confidence. Misleading assumptions can send them on a wild goose chase to build products that nobody needs. Great user interviews are the result of proper planning—whether they are in person or remote. In fact, the user research methodology is optimized for remote situations, and many product teams in top companies routinely conduct remote interviews in order to save time and money.

---

[5]Adapted from Tom Uhlhorn, *Conducting Remote Interviews*. https://www.toptal.com/product-managers/remote/remote-user-interviews

THE BASICS

What is a customer interview? A customer interview is a structured conversation with users or customers in order to understand their needs and real-life problems. It can be conducted face to face or remotely on a video-conferencing platform. Top companies choose remote interviews as a solution to save time and money and gain valuable users' insights.

Why is a user interview important? A user interview informs product teams about what is valuable to their users and leads them to build products and features that solve actual problems. A deep understanding of customers' needs is the vital difference between research that will enhance projects and research that will lead you down the wrong path.

Why do user interviews fail? User interviews fail if they are not well prepared for. The biggest portion of preparation is to conceptualize what you are trying to learn from the user. For remote interviews, double-check if the interviewee is aware of the technical requirements, such as a stable internet connection.

How long should user interviews be? The recommended length to interview one user is 30–45 minutes. For a remote interview, take into account that some free video-conferencing tools have certain limits for one call. For example, Zoom's free version has a limit of 40 minutes per call.

What is a customer discovery interview? A customer discovery interview is the process of talking to potential customers with a goal to discover if a business plan will turn into a profitable business. These interviews are conducted before developing a product or service in order to determine if there are actual customers who will use it.

HOW TO CONDUCT REMOTE INTERVIEWS

Remote interviews are more informative to the researcher than face-to-face interviews. People are much better at building rapport with each other through body language, social chitchat, and validating gestures or agreement than through listening. My best research happened when I did not see the interviewee and kept the discussion limited to the project context. When you are in a room observing social norms, it is more difficult to focus on an interview, as research and rapport do not go together.

Therefore, even without the need for social distancing, I am an advocate of remote user research. The essential requirement for virtual meetings is properly functioning technology for both the interviewer and interviewee. Below, I run through the tools that I have implemented with clients all over the world to conduct effective remote user research.

1. Video communications: Zoom, MS Teams, Google Meet, etc., can all be used. You'll see the most success if interviewees can join the meeting from a browser, thus not needing to install the software. I recommend scheduling an interview for 30–45 minutes. Let the interviewee know that they may turn the video off and explain the reason behind it: You will focus on listening and taking notes and will not be able to look at the interviewee's face.

2. Interview tracker: Keeping notes and identifying key takeaways from your interviews helps you focus on your user's perspective. My usual sample size for the discovery stage is 15 interviews per problem area. Exceeding that number may result in wasted time and energy.

APPENDIX H: PROBLEM CURATION AND DISCOVERY TIPS AND QUESTIONS

This appendix provides tips on how to make your conversations in steps 2 (curation) and 3 (discovery) of the Innovation Pipeline as productive as possible to save you and your agency time and to cut down on the frustration end users and stakeholders may experience in getting you up to speed on their problems.

DISCOVERY TIPS

- Baseline your conversations. Ask about the subject's organization, role, and core responsibilities.
- Don't follow a script. Have specific questions in mind but allow the conversation to take unexpected turns.
- Be specific. If you ask vague questions, you'll probably get vague answers. Specific questions are always better. Instead of asking, "What is your problem?" ask, "Do you have a problem with [Insert hypothesis]?"
- Don't sell a solution. Listen and learn from their perspective.
- Don't offer your insights. It's common to want to explain what you know about the subject. Instead, try to understand why the subject has this perspective.
- Dig into conflicting information. Different subjects often provide conflicting perspectives. As above, try to understand why each has that perspective.
- Collect the right amount of input. Discovery isn't over until you have mapped all the stakeholders, the workflow, and you no longer receive new information from each interview you conduct.

QUESTIONS TO HELP YOU GET STARTED

Use these questions as a starting point when formulating your own questions for an interview. Remember to adapt them to the specific person and problem at hand.

- How did this problem come to be or originate?
- What is a specific example of when this problem occurred? Do you have a horror story of a time when it happened?
- Are there other ongoing efforts to solve this problem? Who else is working on it?
- Has anyone attempted to solve this problem previously? Why weren't they successful?
- Who has to deal with this problem most often/is most impacted by it? Why? (Beneficiary)
- What specific thing makes this so hard? Are you missing a tool? Is there an impossible bureaucratic step? (Pain point)
- What would happen if this was solved? How would your life be easier? What else would you be able to accomplish? (Desired outcome)
- Who else can we talk to about this?

APPENDIX I: ASSESSING PROBLEMS AND SOLUTIONS: A STEP-BY-STEP GUIDE

This appendix is an example of a detailed approach to Innovation Pipeline steps 1, 2 and 3: how to gather and assess the problems within your organization and how to begin to develop appropriate solutions for the problems you identify.

ASSESSING PROBLEMS + SOLUTIONS
A STEP-BY-STEP GUIDE

STEP 1: DEFINE THE PROBLEM

We have found the most useful problem statements include beneficiaries, basic needs, and desired outcomes. For the sake of simplicity, we use the following template: *[Beneficiary] needs [Basic Need] in order to [Desired Outcome]*

Action: Select a single problem and write it out using the template.

Example: *Strike Team Commandos need a transformed mobility training solution in order to increase the probability of mission success and survivability.*

STEP 2: FRAME THE OPPORTUNITY

We use the "How Might We" tool that was popularized by IDEO, the world famous innovation agency. This takes the problem and tries to reframe it in a curious, open-ended question that opens our minds to future possibilities.

Action: Take the problem statement and rewrite it as a "How Might We" question on post-its.

Example: *How might we maximize strike team commando driver capabilities?*

STEP 3: VOTE

Now we start the prioritization process. Each team member should receive 3 dot stickers, or you can draw a small circle on the post-it instead. When voting, focus on those ideas that you think are most valuable if they end up working.

Action: Take 5 minutes to review all the solution ideas and vote on your top 3.

STEP 4: PRIORITIZE

This is where we actually start to leave behind some of the less promising ideas. Take an easel sheet, whiteboard, or any square flat surface. Draw and label two axes: x-axis, "Effort" and the y-axis, "Impact." Now you'll physically locate each HMW *relative to the other HMWs*. This is not meant to be an absolute scale. It's only important if an HMW is more/less impactful and requires more/less effort than the others.

Action: Place all the ideas that received at least one vote on this chart, one at a time. Ensure ideas to the left require less effort than those to the right, and the ideas toward the top would have a greater impact than those toward the bottom.

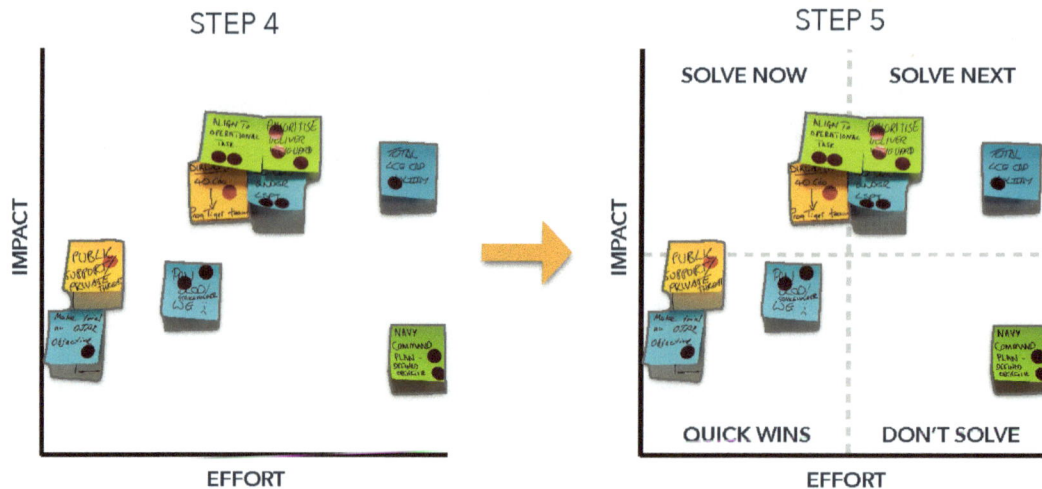

STEP 4 — STEP 5

STEP 5: SELECT

Overlay four quadrants onto the chart. Usually the team will select the idea closest to the top-left part of the Impact/Effort chart. However, sometimes there are other conditions that may not be captured during the process that leads the team to select another idea. That's fine so long as everyone has a chance to discuss and debate the tradeoffs of one over another. What's important is the team selects a single idea and *commits to testing it.*

Action: Decide on a "winning" idea.

STEP 6: GENERATE ASSUMPTIONS

A host of potential issues will pop up as soon as you start thinking through your idea. Capture these and try to identify which category best describes it: user desirability, organizational viability, or technical feasibility. Note, it's possible for assumptions blend two or three categories.

- **Desirability** tests whether the innovation project is solving the right problem.
- **Viability** tests for long-term sustainability.
- **Feasibility** tests whether the idea is technologically possible.

Action: Write down at least 3 assumptions for each category: Desirability (assumptions you're making about users wanting the solution); Feasibility (assumption you're making about what technology can do); and Viability (assumptions you're making about your organization's response to it).

Assumption Examples (from Example Problem Statement in Step 1):

- *Desirability: Synthetic training environment will aid mobility training*
- *Feasibility: Data to build the synthetic environment exists*
- *Viability: External training enablers can be found and funded in time (6-12 weeks)*

STEP 7: DEVELOP QUESTIONS

Now we need to figure out how to validate these assumptions. We want to develop a list of questions that cover our most important assumptions so we can test them now, rather than find out later we were wrong about one (or more) of them. This requires us to ask specific questions to specific kinds of people. It's important that we avoid these mistakes:

(1) asking people if they like our idea; or

(2) asking people questions outside their area of expertise, causing them to speculate.

Action: Write down at least one question for each assumption, capturing them in a single document.

Examples (from above assumptions):

- *Desirability*
  - *Tell me about your current driver training course.*
  - *How closely do you think it mimics a real-world operating environment?*
  - *Would you be open to using a simulated training environment if it required you to use a VR headset?*
  - *How well does your current driver training prepare you for real-world operations?*
- *Feasibility*
  - *What software have you seen that builds a map based on collected imagery?*
  - *Have you seen any companies that take this data and builds a simulated or immersive experience?*
  - *How do video game companies build a simulated environment?*
  - *Do we have any satellite imagery or map data in-house that can be used to build a simulated environment?*
- *Viability*
  - *Does our organization have any VR headsets right now that we could use?*
  - *Are we able to buy a software license for quick testing in a sandbox (off-network) environment? Who approves requests like this?*
  - *Are funds available to purchase a software license for a limited duration experiment?*

STEP 8: IDENTIFY BENEFICIARIES

Now your team needs to start using its network. We want to find people who have opinions based on experience, training, and education. They can be technical experts, operators/end-users, program managers, or key stakeholders (e.g. security officer, financial officer). Identify individuals *by name or specific position*, not just notionally.

Action: Write down at least 3 experts or users to interview for each assumption.

STEP 9: INTERVIEW

Setting up and conducting interviews should be straightforward. Reach out to each person to schedule a time to speak with him or her. Face-to-face is preferred but not necessary to get valuable feedback. Ensure there are at least two people from your team at each interview, one to ask the questions and one to take notes. Whenever another organization or person is mentioned, try to get contact information. Ideally you'll also get the interviewee to introduce you to that next expert or user. Most importantly, ask open-ended questions that will help you get into the mind set of your interviewee, avoid "yes" or "no" questions, and make sure to focus on validating (or invalidating) the assumptions you generated in Step 6.

Action: Conduct interviews, keeping all of your notes in a central location.

STEP 10: ANALYZE & ADJUST

The team should briefly review the answers to their questions after each interview. Initially this review might take 15-20 minutes, but it will shrink to a 5 minute exercise if done enough. The team should consider what they learned, *particularly if an assumption appears to be invalidated*. If so, make sure to speak with at least 2 more users or experts about that assumption. If you get the same answer consistently, then should revisit your solution and figure out if you need to change the idea. It helps to use the software "versioning" system (e.g. 1.0, 1.1, 2.0, 2.1) to annotate your solutions. Small changes are indicated as 1.0 to 1.1, whereas large changes are indicated as 1.0 to 2.0.

Action: Track validated and invalidated assumptions, noting when the solution idea changes and which conversations led to that change.

APPENDIX J: MISSION MODEL CANVAS

This appendix supports step 3, discovery, in creating and delivering mission impact to your end users. Use this tool to test your hypotheses about possible problem solutions in order to validate your project.

The Mission Model Canvas (MMC) is an important tool to generate hypotheses about how to create and deliver value to the government end user. Use this tool to test all of your hypotheses in order to validate and de-risk your project. When completed, the MMC fits tidily onto one page (example below). The MMC will change as you talk to end users, beneficiaries, key partners, and other stakeholders. Changing the MMC is a sign of progress, not failure. It means you are learning from real-world testing.

Once each hypothesis is validated, the MMC will show that customers want to use your solution, that it is technically possible to build your solution, and that the organization will support its adoption and deployment.

The Mission Model Canvas — blank template with sections: Key Partners, Key Activities, Key Resources, Value Propositions, Buy-in & Support, Deployment, Beneficiaries, Mission Budget/Cost, Mission Achievement/Impact Factors. Designed by: Strategyzer AG & Steve Blank, The makers of Business Model Generation and Strategyzer. Strategyzer / strategyzer.com

How Do I Use the MMC?

Answer the questions within each box relevant to one specific problem/solution. Then note each answer that is validated. If it is not validated, it is an assumption! To decrease the risk and increase your confidence in your project, you must validate each hypothesis. If your hypotheses change, re-validate each previously validated hypothesis.

The Mission Model Canvas

Mission/Problem Description: Designed by: Date: Version:

Key Partners	Key Activities	Value Propositions	Buy-in & Support	Beneficiaries
Which Key Activities can/must you outsource? **To whom?**	What activities need to be completed in order to deliver the Value Proposition?	What are you offering the beneficiaries? What problem are you solving for them? What pains does your solution solve for them? What gains do you give them?	Whose buy-in is needed to deploy the product? What is required to support it once deployed?	Who are the individuals you are creating value for? What jobs do they really want to get done? Differentiate between target/tangential and direct/up or down stream beneficiaries.

Key Resources

Which internal resources do you need to perform the activities? What must be done in-house?

Deployment

What will it take to deploy the product / service from the current MVP to widespread use?

Mission Budget/Cost

How much does it cost to deliver the value proposition? Which key elements drive your costs?

How will the timeline of deployment affect the timing of financial resources?

Mission Achievement/Impact Factors

How do your beneficiaries measure achievement? How do they know they've succeeded?

How do those you need Buy-in + Support from measure mission achievement?

APPENDIX K: VALUE PROPOSITION CANVAS

This appendix supports step 3, discovery, with a template for determining the value proposition that your problems and potential solutions may hold for the end user.

To complete this template, you will create two conclusions:
- Who/what is the precise end user (customer segment) you are addressing?
- What is the value proposition of a solution you can deliver to your end user to address their problems and to either solve the pain points associated with that problem or increase their mission results or satisfaction?

To first develop the customer segment (circle below), itemize:
- the range of jobs that your end user (customer) performs
- challenges or pains the end user experiences in doing these jobs
- ways the end user experiences gains or increases mission results or satisfaction

To then develop the value proposition (box below), itemize:
- possible products and services that could address the end user's problems
- possible ways to reduce the end user's challenges (or pain relievers) with a potential solution
- possible ways to increase the end user's satisfaction (gain creators) with a potential solution

Use the derived value proposition to evaluate proposed solutions to your end user problems. The Value Proposition Canvas is also critical in completing the Mission Model Canvas (Appendix J).

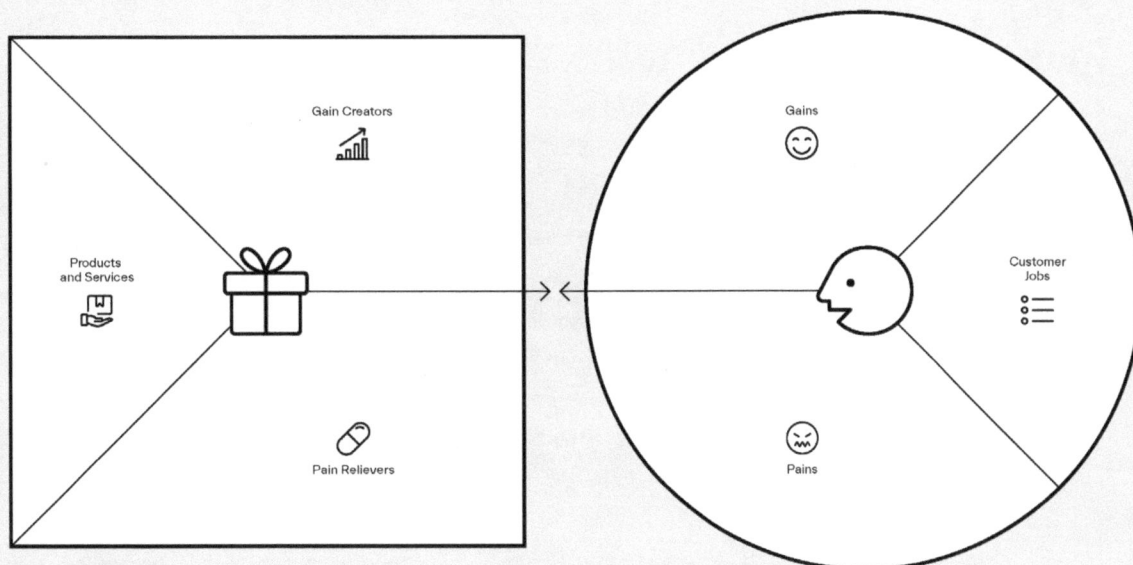

The Value Proposition Canvas

Gain Creators

Products and Services

Pain Relievers

Gains

Customer Jobs

Pains

Copyright: Strategyzer AG
The makers of Business Model Generation and Strategyzer

⟲ Strategyzer
strategyzer.com

APPENDIX L: ASSESSING TECHNOLOGY PROGRESS TOWARD DEPLOYMENT

This appendix supports steps 4 (incubate) and 5 (transition) with an assessment for proposed solution readiness and maturity to solve mission problems, to meet your mission priorities, and to create mission impact. Note that this assessment is primarily intended to evaluate the readiness of a technology solution for transition, but with some modification it can be used to evaluate any type of solution, whether involving strategies, policies, processes, or communications.

ASSESSING PROGRESS TOWARD DEPLOYMENT
INVESTMENT AND ADOPTION READINESS LEVELS

WHY MEASURE READINESS LEVELS?

Readiness levels are tools to measure and communicate your project's progress toward deployment. Each level is data-driven and evidenced-based, providing a more concrete way to demonstrate desirability, feasibility, and viability. Each readiness level measures the:

- **Technology Readiness Level (TRL):** *feasibility* of your project's technical operationalization
- **Investment Readiness Level (IRL):** *desirability* for key partners to commit resources (time, money, equipment, manpower) to your project
- **Adoption Readiness Level (ARL):** organizational *viability* to deploy + sustain your project

HOW TO MEASURE READINESS LEVELS

Pages 2-3 offer a lightweight rubric to assess your project's IRL and ARL. There are tasks to complete and questions to ask; your project has successfully achieved each level when you have done both. When you reach a "critical gate," you cannot make any more progress until you can answer that question affirmatively.

WHEN TO MEASURE READINESS LEVELS

ARL assessment generally begins around the time your project has reached IRL 5 or 6. The initial stages of ARL assessment coincide with some stages of IRL assessment. See below.

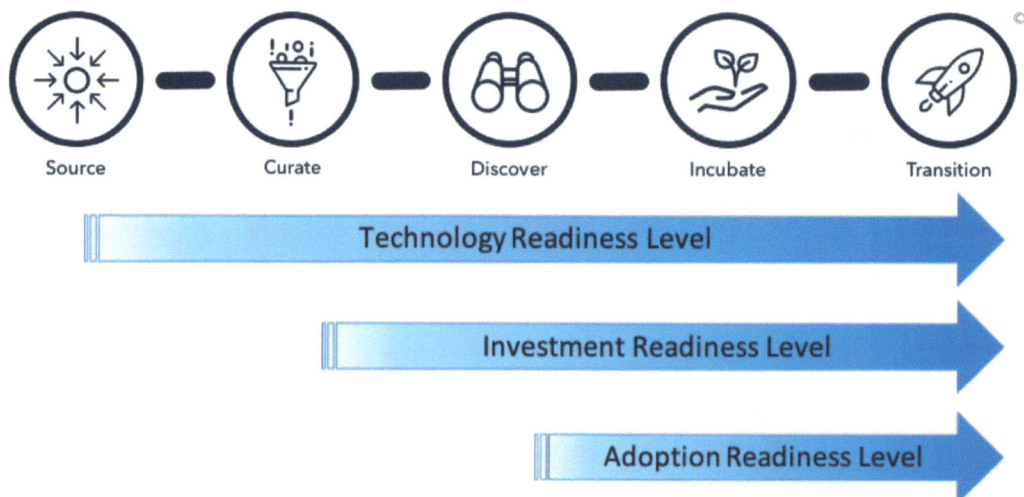

| Source | Curate | Discover | Incubate | Transition |

Technology Readiness Level

Investment Readiness Level

Adoption Readiness Level

INVESTMENT READINESS LEVEL (IRL)

Self-Assessment

IRL	IRL Stage	Funding Stage	Tasks to Complete	Questions to Ask
1	Understand problem		Understand problem	What problem am I trying to solve? What are beneficiary pain points? Have I formed critical assumptions around desirability, feasibility, and viability?
2	1st Mission Model Canvas (MMC)		Complete MMC	Does the solution align to beneficiary pain points? What is the value proposition? Who are the beneficiaries? What are key activities, key partners, and key resources? How will it be deployed? What buy-in and support is needed? What is the mission budget and cost? What is the mission impact?
3	Value proposition and beneficiary defined, problem/ solution validation	SBIR/STTR phase I ready	Value proposition and beneficiary defined, problem/solution validation	Is there a clear beneficiary and a value proposition? Has the beneficiary validated the problem and the proposed solution?
4	First Low Fidelity MVP	Pre-Seed investment ready	First low fidelity MVP	Does the MVP (inexpensive, easy to use, and relevant) solve beneficiary pain points? What am I learning during testing to improve the MVP?
5	Mission Model Canvas & team		Mission Model Canvas (MMC), competitive landscape, early team	Does this solution help the beneficiary achieve mission impact for their organization? Who can help me build this solution?
6	Preliminary Product Market Fit (PMF), validated competitive landscape	Seed investment / SBIR/STTR phase II ready	Preliminary PMF, validated competitive landscape	Have beneficiaries validated this solution in delivering mission impact? Is this more effective than the competition in doing so?
7	Initial product plan and key activities		Initial product plan; key development and activities validated	What have I learned from previous testing and customer discovery that can be applied to the solution? What elements are critical in the solution to addressing key pain points?
8	Prototype High Fidelity MVP		Prototype high fidelity MVP	What agreements, accreditations, or authorities do I need to deploy the solution? What partnerships are critical to its success?
9	Investment ready, initial team, market, tech, traction	Post-Seed ready / SBIR/STTR III ready	Early traction, team, tech validate market pitch deck	What are my validated funding sources? What is my deployment plan that the beneficiary has validated?

ADOPTION READINESS LEVEL (ARL)

Self-Assessment

ARL	TASKS TO COMPLETE	QUESTIONS TO ASK
1	Confirm a committed problem owner and senior leader support	Can I clearly explain the problem I'm solving to someone else? Have I found someone who is willing to work on this for the next ~6 months?
2	Identify key stakeholders and funding sources	Have I identified someone with sufficient resources to fund my proof-of-concept?
3	Identify contracting pathways and confirm stakeholder support	Have my key stakeholders agreed to advocate for my proposed solution? Have I identified a contractual pathway for my solution (if applicable)?
4	Seek feedback on your proposed solution and get approval to use contractual pathway (if applicable)	Have I gotten feedback on my proposed solution from key stakeholders? If a contracted third party will build my solution, have they received approval to engage the identified contractual pathway?
5	Confirm commitment from long-term resource sponsor and readiness to build proof-of-concept	Has my long-term resource sponsor formally committed to a partnership? Do I have the resources needed to conduct or construct an initial proof-of-concept?
6	Get approval and funding to conduct pilots	Has my long-term resource sponsor approved and identified funding to run field trials of my solution?
7	Test your solution in a comprehensive integrated trial within a representative system	Has my long-term resource sponsor given me approval and funding for a trial of my integrated solution in a representative system?
8	Get approval and funding for your transition plan, including acquisition and maintenance	Has my long-term resource sponsor approved and funded a plan to acquire my solution?
9	Transition the solution to the long-term owner for maintenance	Has my solution transitioned to my long-term resource sponsor?

- **IRL 9** — Investment ready, initial team, market, tech, traction
- **IRL 8** — Prototype High Fidelity MVP
- **IRL 7** — Initial product plan and key activities
- **IRL 6** — Preliminary Product Market Fit (PMF), validated competitive landscape
- **IRL 5** — Mission Model Canvas & team
- **IRL 4** — First Low Fidelity MVP
- **IRL 3** — Value proposition and beneficiary defined, problem/solution validation
- **IRL 2** — First Mission Model Canvas (MMC)
- **IRL 1** — Understand problem

- **ARL 9** — Capability transitioned to long-term resource sponsor
- **ARL 8** — Acquisition and sustainment plan for capability funded by long-term resource sponsor
- **ARL 7** — Systems representative trial of integrated capability funded by long-term resource sponsor
- **ARL 6** — Successful pilots funded by long-term resource sponsor, additional letters of intent and/or requests for integration
- **ARL 5** — Successful Proof of Concept funded by initial resource sponsor, letter of intent from long-term resouce sponsor
- **ARL 4** — Key stakeholder feedback on proposed capability, solution provider(s) contractually engaged
- **ARL 3** — Key stakeholder commitment, validation of critical assumptions, contractual pathway determined
- **ARL 2** — Critical assumptions and key stakeholders identified, initial funding source identified
- **ARL 1** — Basic problem identified and summarized

APPENDIX M: CREATING A TRANSITION AGREEMENT

This appendix will help you craft a successful technology transition plan and agreement, ensuring a smooth shift from step 4 (incubation) to step 5 (transition) and a clear and common understanding of how the transition will take place. Although this guide is meant specifically for a technology transition, it can be used to move any initial solution, whether policy, process, or other solution, into an operational capacity.

In general, transition plans should have the following elements:

- A development outline, describing the development pathway of the technology or other solution in detail
- Expected outcomes of the project. The outcomes should be measurable and achievable "exit criteria."
- Funding strategy. The strategy names the resources to be provided according to source, appropriation, program element, amount, and timing.
- Identified customer, schedule, and milestones, including a transition or handoff schedule
- Acquisition strategy, fielding, and integration plan
- Issues and risks for cost, schedule, technical, manufacturability, sustainment
- Signed "customer" and program manager agreement for funding, schedule, and deliverables
- Plan from multiple sources for using the technology or other solution and encouraging innovation

TRANSITION AGREEMENT

Introduction

- Purpose/Scope. Provide a brief statement. [Example: The Program Manager and S&T Organization mutually agree to enter into this Technology Transition Agreement (TTA) for the purpose of defining technology deliverables from the appropriate name technologies development program, to appropriate name program. This TTA defines the functional responsibilities and support relationships between the parties signing this agreement. It ensures a clear understanding of the responsibilities of all parties to ensure a successful transition of technology from S&T organization to the program of record name.]
- Summary. Provide a brief overview , two to three paragraphs in length, summarizing what this project will provide to the program of record. Include an explanation of the current situation (usually expressed as a problem or shortcoming) and what funding (list funding amount) will be used in bringing a corrective solution to fruition. Include the causes or reasons for the current problem/predicament. Describe the impact of the problem in terms of reduced operational effectiveness (e.g., warfighting capability or mission accomplishment) or efficiency (e.g., total ownership cost). Justify the reason(s) for a technology insertion outside the normal POM cycle. Describe the seminal Transition Event and when it will happen. Also provide the number of units (or some other quantitative metric) that will be procured with the new technology transitioned. Indicate the consequence or alternative action to be taken if the transition funding is not implemented (what is your plan B to get the solution transitioned).

Basic Transition Agreement

- Technology Name. Name or names of the technology to be transitioned. Description of the technology to be delivered. Include all aliases, prior names, STO numbers, or other identifying numbers or acronyms. Indicate if the technology is only a subset of the underlying STO or S&T program.
- Description of Technology or Capability to Be Delivered. Specific, technical description of what the S&T Program or Source-Program Manager intends to develop for transition to the primary acquisition program, including numbers of prototypes or test items. The description should include delivery dates, delivery mechanism (purchase, loan, given to program, etc.) and specific exit criteria concerning the capability to be available at each delivery date. Identify project objectives for each fiscal year's funding as well as the outcomes to be achieved with that funding.

- Target Acquisition Program. Brief description of the acquisition program intended to receive the technology. Include major program objectives, ACAT level, current phase of acquisition life cycle, next milestone decision review (and anticipated date), and projected initial operational capability date.
- Acquisition Program Technology Need. Brief description of the benefit that this technology will bring to the acquisition program or need satisfied. Identify the technology needs of the acquisition program that S&T is expected to provide.
  - Relate the benefit to the Initial Capabilities Document (ICD) , Capability Development Document (CDD), Key Performance Parameters (KPP), etc.
  - Include need dates for specific capabilities.
  - Provide an estimate of the technology readiness level (TRL) for each technology/product need identified utilizing a systems approach for hardware and software as the measure of technical maturity and indication of transition readiness. Coordinate the TRL with the S&T activity.
- Integration Strategy. Describe the process for integrating the technology into the acquisition program. Include the following elements of the acquisition strategy:
  - Evolutionary acquisition, block upgrade, etc.
  - Required contractor-to-contractor agreements
  - Acquisition appropriation and Program Element (PE) numbers funding the transition
  - Annual PE funding levels committed to the transition program
  - Transition FY
  - Statement conveying the level of commitment. For example
    - Commitment [Example: "Upon successful demonstration of key performance requirements (exit criteria), appropriate name acquisition program office will integrate XXX (product S&T organization will deliver) into appropriate name (acquisition program that will integrate the deliverable) commencing in FYXX (transition year)." This integration effort will be funded under PE XXXXXXX, Project XXXX (FYDP budget profile for this acquisition line should be included).]
    - Intent [Example: Upon successful demonstration of key performance requirements (exit criteria), appropriate name (acquisition program office) intends to integrate XXX (product S&T organization is delivering) into appropriate name (acquisition program that will integrate the deliverable) commencing in FYXX (transition year) under PE XXXXXXX Project XXXX (FYDP budget profile).]
- Program Manager/Project Officer. Identify the program manager and the individual in the program office responsible for day-to-day management, with contact information, concerning the technology.
- Technology Manager. Identify the individual designated by either the S&T activity or the source technology program office, PM, or PEO to coordinate and manage daily development of the technology.
- Capability Requirement Basis. Identify the governing source of the capability requirement: the ICD, CDD, or other official reference documenting the capability need.
- Resource Sponsor/Requirements Officer. Identify the resource sponsor and requirements officer responsible for resourcing and establishing requirements for the capability. Include contact information.

Technical Details And Programmatics
- Current Status of Technology.
  - Status Summary. Summarize the current state of the development of the technology. Identify primary areas where additional development is required. Provide estimate of current technology readiness level (TRL) ratings. Indicate if an independent analysis of the TRL has been performed, and if so, provide a summary of that analysis.
  - Risk Analysis. Major areas of risk, prioritized, with planned mitigation activities. Include technical, producibility, affordability, sustainability, cost, and schedule risks.
- Technology Development Strategy. Outline planned approach. Describe current efforts and efforts required beyond those currently underway. Detail integration plans if multiple projects are planned. Include planned ATD or ACTD developments, if applicable.

- Key Measures of Transition Readiness. Identify the key parameters or attributes that will be used as exit criteria to measure whether or not the technology effort is proceeding as scheduled. Include parameters to be tracked, current state, interim progress estimates, and final objective. TRLs are a measure of technical maturity and can be used to assess readiness to transition. Provide dates when each higher TRL rating is expected to be achieved.
- Program Plan. Show major activities/efforts of the technology development activity, with milestones. Provide a schedule with all pertinent information.
- Funding Adequacy. State and agree that the combined sources of all funding are adequate to achieve the maturity and quantity of the technology required by the receiving PM in the time frame(s) required by the PM and as specified in this document.

Reporting Requirements
- The Program Manager will provide a semi-annual technical status to the TTI Office no later than 30 June and 31 December, a transition report to the TTI Office within 60 days of the transition event, and a final letter report to the TTI Office within 30 days of fielding the technology.
- The Technology Manager will provide monthly TTI funds execution status reports to the TTI Office NLT the 28th day of each month.
- The FY06 Appropriations Act included language that requires a quarterly report for the TTI Program. The Technology Manager will provide the necessary inputs for that report.

Signatures
Excerpted from *Manager's Guide to Technology Transition in an Evolutionary Acquisition Environment*, Appendix D, Office of the Undersecretary of Defense (Acquisition, Technology & Logistics), 2012.

APPENDIX N: PROBLEM AND SOLUTIONS PROGRESS MAP AND SCORING MATRIX

This appendix provides a process, documentation, and metrics to ensure each potential solution for identified problems has documented rigor behind it.

WEEK	TASKS TO COMPLETE	IDEAL ACHIEVEMENT	TEAM 1	TEAM 2	TEAM 3	TEAM 4	TEAM 5
1	VALIDATE THE BENEFICIARY	50					
1	VALIDATE THE PAIN POINT	50					
1	VALIDATE THE DESIRED OUTCOME	50					
2	DEVELOP AND PRIORITIZE ONE SOLUTION IDEA THAT CAN SOLVE THE BENEFICIARY'S PROBLEM	50					
2	COLLECT SOME INITIAL ASSUMPTIONS THAT MUST BE TRUE FOR YOUR SOLUTION TO ADDRESS THE PROBLEM	50					
SLB 1	"MY PROBLEM IS REAL AND MY SOLUTION IDEA MAKES SENSE TO SOLVE IT."	250					
3	FORM DESIRABILITY HYPOTHESES	25					
3	FORM FEASIBILITY HYPOTHESES	25					
3	FORM VIABILITY HYPOTHESES	25					
3	VALIDATE THE PROBLEM WITH THOSE EXPERIENCING IT	50					
3	VALIDATE THAT YOUR SOLUTION ADDRESSES YOUR USER'S PROBLEM	50					
3	IDENTIFY WHAT YOU WILL MEASURE TO INDICATE WHETHER OR NOT IT ADDRESSES THE PROBLEM	25					
4 - 5	TEST ONE HYPOTHESIS ABOUT YOUR SOLUTION WITH THOSE EXPERIENCING THE PROBLEM	25					
4 - 5	DETERMINE WHETHER OR NOT IT MEETS THE VALIDATION CRITERIA	25					
4 - 5	DETERMINE NEXT ITEMS TO TEST	25					
4 - 5	REPEAT UNTIL DESIRABILITY IS VALIDATED	50					
4 - 5	TEST YOUR HYPOTHESES ABOUT YOUR SOLUTION WITH EXPERTS WHO CAN HELP YOU BUILD IT	25					
4 - 5	DETERMINE WHETHER OR NOT THEY MEET THE VALIDATION CRITERIA	25					
4 - 5	DETERMINE NEXT ITEMS TO TEST	25					
4 - 5	REPEAT UNTIL FEASIBILITY IS VALIDATED	50					

WEEK	TASKS TO COMPLETE	IDEAL ACHIEVEMENT	TEAM 1	TEAM 2	TEAM 3	TEAM 4	TEAM 5
4 - 5	TEST ONE HYPOTHESIS ABOUT YOUR SOLUTION WITH KEY PARTNERS	25					
4 - 5	DETERMINE WHETHER OR NOT IT MEETS THE VALIDATION CRITERIA	25					
4 - 5	DETERMINE NEXT ITEMS TO TEST	25					
4 - 5	REPEAT UNTIL VIABILITY IS VALIDATED	50					
5	DEFINE HOW YOUR SOLUTION IDEA ALIGNS TO STRATEGIC / MISSION IMPERATIVES	50					
5	BUILD PRESENTATION	50					
5	OUTLINE VALIDATION + RECOMMENDATIONS	75					
SLB 2	"I KNOW WHAT TO BUILD."	1000					
EXTRA	IDENTIFY HOW MUCH IT WILL COST TO BUILD AND DEPLOY THIS SOLUTION	50					
EXTRA	IDENTIFY WHO CAN HELP YOU BUILD AND DEPLOY THIS SOLUTION	50					
EXTRA	IDENTIFY WHO WILL FUND BUILDING AND DEPLOYING THIS SOLUTION	50					
	TOTAL	1150					

PROJECT LEAD: EACH WEEK, MANUALLY ENTER THE ROW TOTALS

WEEK 1 TOTAL	
WEEK 2 TOTAL	
WEEK 3 TOTAL	
WEEK 4 TOTAL	
WEEK 5 TOTAL	

APPENDIX O: PERIODIC INNOVATION PIPELINE ASSESSMENT

This appendix is a matrix for benchmarking the elements of the Innovation Pipeline (see Appendix A) and the activities within each step to measure success and ensure the pipeline is moving toward realizing innovation for your organization. Use it to assess your organization's capacity to innovate, highlight areas that impede innovation, and inform decisions about what, where, and how the organization can change to meet strategic mission imperatives.

INNOVATION PIPELINE SELF ASSESSMENT KEY

Strategy

- What's the goal for the Team
- What's the goal for Leadership

Pipeline & Infrastructure Process

Process
- What's the input and where does it come from?
- What's the output (deliverable product of this step)?

Team / Resources
- What team and what expertise is needed?
- What resources are required (funding, contracts, exceptions)

Operational Support

- Type of organizational support required (contracts, HR, Security)
- What leadership is required (resource/compliance decisions, firefighting etc)

Activities, Methodologies, Tools and Metrics

Activities and Methodologies
- What methodologies are used to perform this step
- Skills required and experiences needed

Tools and Skills
- Tools applied to collect insight
- Skills need to enable execution

Data and Assessments
- What metrics are used to measure throughput
- What vital signs (data) are used to check performance

SOURCE

Teams' goals are defined Score ☐	**Leaderships' goal is defined** Score ☐
Appropriate input is available Score ☐	**Output is generated to drive next step** Score ☐
Team & expertise is available Score ☐	**Resources are available** Score ☐
Organizational support is available Score ☐	**Leadership available & decisions points identified** Score ☐
Activities executed to generate output Score ☐	**Methodologies defined/used to guide discovery** Score ☐
Tools defined to collect insight Score ☐	**Training provide to develop execution skills** Score ☐
Metrics are defined to determine success Score ☐	**Data is collected to measure vital signs** Score ☐

1 – Exceptional. 2 – Adequate, requires constant oversight. 3 – Non-existent or not available

*Higher scores reflect increasing risk

*Total Score ☐

CURATE

Teams' goals are defined	Leaderships' goal is defined
Score	Score

Appropriate input is available	Output is generated to drive next step
Score	Score

Team & expertise is available	Resources are available
Score	Score

Organizational support is available	Leadership available & decisions points identified
Score	Score

Activities executed to generate output	Methodologies defined/used to guide discovery
Score	Score

Tools defined to collect insight	Training provide to develop execution skills
Score	Score

Metrics are defined to determine success	Data is collected to measure vital signs
Score	Score

1 – Exceptional. 2 – Adequate, requires constant oversight. 3 – Non-existent or not available

*Higher scores reflect increasing risk

*Total Score

DISCOVER

Teams' goals are defined		Leaderships' goal is defined	
	Score		Score

Appropriate input is available		Output is generated to drive next step	
	Score		Score

Team & expertise is available		Resources are available	
	Score		Score

Organizational support is available		Leadership available & decisions points identified	
	Score		Score

Activities executed to generate output		Methodologies defined/used to guide discovery	
	Score		Score

Tools defined to collect insight		Training provide to develop execution skills	
	Score		Score

Metrics are defined to determine success		Data is collected to measure vital signs	
	Score		Score

1 – Exceptional. 2 – Adequate, requires constant oversight. 3 – Non-existent or not available

*Higher scores reflect increasing risk

*Total
Score

INCUBATE

Teams' goals are defined Score ☐	**Leaderships' goal is defined** Score ☐
Appropriate input is available Score ☐	**Output is generated to drive next step** Score ☐
Team & expertise is available Score ☐	**Resources are available** Score ☐
Organizational support is available Score ☐	**Leadership available & decisions points identified** Score ☐
Activities executed to generate output Score ☐	**Methodologies defined/used to guide discovery** Score ☐
Tools defined to collect insight Score ☐	**Training provide to develop execution skills** Score ☐
Metrics are defined to determine success Score ☐	**Data is collected to measure vital signs** Score ☐

1 – Exceptional. 2 – Adequate, requires constant oversight. 3 – Non-existent or not available

*Higher scores reflect increasing risk

*Total Score ☐

TRANSITION

| Teams' goals are defined | Leaderships' goal is defined |
| Score | Score |

| Appropriate input is available | Output is generated to drive next step |
| Score | Score |

| Team & expertise is available | Resources are available |
| Score | Score |

| Organizational support is available | Leadership available & decisions points identified |
| Score | Score |

| Activities executed to generate output | Methodologies defined/used to guide discovery |
| Score | Score |

| Tools defined to collect insight | Training provide to develop execution skills |
| Score | Score |

| Metrics are defined to determine success | Data is collected to measure vital signs |
| Score | Score |

1 – Exceptional. 2 – Adequate, requires constant oversight. 3 – Non-existent or not available

*Higher scores reflect increasing risk

*Total Score

RESOURCES

Blank, Steve. *The Four Steps to the Epiphany: Successful Strategies for Products That Win*, 5th edition. Hoboken, NJ: John C. Wiley & Sons, Inc., 2020.

Blank, Steve. *How to Avoid Innovation Theater: The Six Decisions to Make Before Establishing an Innovation Outpost*. Blog post, December 15, 2015.

Blank, Steve, and Bob Dorf. *The Startup Owner's Manual: The Step-by-Step Guide for Building a Great Company*. Pescadero, CA: K&S Ranch, 2012.

Catmull, Ed. *Creativity, Inc.: Overcoming the Unseen Forces That Stand in the Way of True Inspiration*. New York: Random House, 2014.

Denning, Peter, and Robert Dunham. *The Innovator's Way: Essential Practices for Successful Innovation*. Cambridge, MA: The MIT Press, 2010.

Fitzpatrick, R. *The Mom Test: How to Talk to Customers and Learn If Your Business Is a Good Idea When Everyone Is Lying To You*. CreateSpace Independent Publishing Platform, 2013.

Isaacson, Walter. *The Innovators: How a Group of Hackers, Geniuses, and Geeks Created the Digital Revolution*. New York: Simon and Schuster, 2014.

Kelley, Tom, and David Kelly. *Creating Confidence: Unleashing the Creative Potential Within Us All*. New York: Random House, 2013.

Larkin, Gregory. *This Might Get Me Fired: A Manual for Thriving in the Corporate Entrepreneurial Underground*. New York: Lioncrest Publishing, 2018.

Liedtka, Jeanne, and Tim Ogilvie. *Designing for Growth: A Design Thinking Toolkit for Managers*. New York: Columbia Business School Publishing, 2011.

Liedtka, Jeanne, Tim Ogilvie, and Rachel Brozenske. *The Designing for Growth Field Book: A Step-by-Step Project Guide*, 2nd edition. New York: Columbia Business School Publishing, 2019.

MacKenzie, Gordon. *Orbiting the Giant Hairball: A Corporate Fool's Guide to Surviving with Grace*. New York: Viking Publishing, 1998.

O'Reilly, III, Charles, and Michael Tushman. *Lead and Disrupt: How to Solve the Innovator's Dilemma*, 2nd edition. Stanford, CA: Stanford University Press, 2021.

Osterwalder, Alexander, and Yves Pigneur. *Business Model Generation*. Hoboken, NJ: John C. Wiley & Sons Inc., 2010.

Osterwalder, Alexander, Yves Pigneur, Greg Barnarda, and Alan Smith. *Value Proposition Design*. Hoboken, NJ: John C. Wiley & Sons Inc., 2020.

Ries, Eric. *The Lean Startup: How Today's Entrepreneurs Use Continuous Innovation to Create Radically Successful Businesses*. New York: Random House, 2011.

Weiss, Mitchell. *We the Possibility: Harnessing Public Entrepreneurship to Solve Our Most Urgent Problems*. Boston, MA: Harvard Business Review Press, 2021.

INDEX